Jane Austen's Guide to Thrift

Jane Austen's Guide to Thrift

AN INDEPENDENT WOMAN'S ADVICE ON LIVING WITHIN ONE'S MEANS

Kathleen Anderson and Susan Jones

BERKLEY BOOKS, NEW YORK

THE BERKLEY PUBLISHING GROUP
Published by the Penguin Group
Penguin Group (USA) Inc.
375 Hudson Street, New York, New York 10014, USA

USA / Canada / UK / Ireland / Australia / New Zealand / India / South Africa / China

Penguin Books Ltd., Registered Offices: 80 Strand, London WC2R 0RL, England
For more information about the Penguin Group, visit penguin.com

This book is an original publication of The Berkley Publishing Group.

Library of Congress Cataloging-in-Publication Data

Anderson, Kathleen.
Jane Austen's guide to thrift / by Kathleen Anderson and Susan Jones.
p. cm.
ISBN 978-0-425-26016-6
1. Home economics.   2. Consumer education.   3. Thriftiness.
4. Austen, Jane, 1775–1817—Characters.   I. Jones, Susan.   II. Title.
TX147.A634 2013
640.73—dc23
2012043437

PUBLISHING HISTORY
Berkley trade paperback edition / April 2013

PRINTED IN THE UNITED STATES OF AMERICA

10 9 8 7 6 5 4 3 2 1

Cover design by Lesley Worrell.
Cover art by Natasha Molotkova.
Book design by Tiffany Estreicher.

To David Athey with love.
Thanks for twenty-two years of thrifty adventures.
—Kathleen Anderson

To my sister, Lisbeth, who is the other half of my self,
and my dear friend Linda Moody, who has put up with
me more times than I can count.
—Susan Jones

Contents

Introduction

Jane Austen's Thrifty Spirit

"I am determined to spend no more . . ."

We love Jane Austen!

Austen's spirited characters and her solid, practical values are as alive to us today as they were in her own time. The more we read her work and enter her world, the more we learn about ourselves. And we wonder what Jane would make of our world and our times, when diets and personal trainers swear they will help us become as thin as supermodels—for a fee. When fashion statements lure us to buy accessories and garments we "can't do without," and to buy them NOW. And when computer pop-ups promise to find our perfect match, if only we fill out a questionnaire and make an online payment.

We wonder: Would Jane Austen or her characters have succumbed to personal trainers to achieve a svelte look? Would Catherine Morland of *Northanger Abbey* pore over fashion magazines and think that a pair of $400 shoes was money well spent? Would *Pride and Prejudice*'s Elizabeth Bennet have turned to an online matchmaking service, looking for Mr. Darcy? Would she have looked in the mirror and pulled out her credit card? We don't think so—Austen had a thrifty spirit that she exhibited both through her most beloved (and even some of her rather loathed) characters. Just look at the number of times money is an issue to her characters. Remember in *Sense and Sensibility* when Marianne Dashwood cries, exuberant as always, "What have wealth and grandeur to do with happiness?" and Elinor argues that wealth may assist a person to be happy. But it is Marianne who has the last word: "Money can only give happiness where there is nothing else to give it. Beyond a competence, it can afford no real satisfaction . . ." Then there's Catherine Morland, who must figure out how much money she should have for her trip to Bath. And we see how important it is for the Bennet sisters, for Harriet Smith of *Emma*, for Anne Elliot of *Persuasion*, for all the Austen heroines to find Mr. Right with the right income, in order to survive.

How else do we know Austen's take on thrift? It is woven through her letters to her sister, Cassandra, which reveal just how often they both had to practice discipline in spending. Austen wrote frequently to her sister about everyday matters, and although Cassandra destroyed many of the letters when Jane died, about 160 of them remain today, in various locations such as the Morgan Library in New York and the National Library of Scotland, so we may share her experiences and ideas. Considering the many ways Jane Austen chose to comment on economics and handling money in both her fiction and her personal writing, it's clear that she has serious opinions on thriving on thrifty living.

When Jane Austen died, having authored six extraordinary novels, she left a small monetary legacy. As a woman, she had never had access to the two main means of acquiring wealth during her time: inheritance or profession. And unlike her characters, she never married into money. Her family never sent her to India to troll for a nabob, an Englishman who founded his family fortune in Far East trading, nor did she long for a planter from the Indies. When we consider Jane Austen's wealth, we see that it lay in herself, in the generosity with which she shared her wit in her letters and publications. As her readers (whether newcomers or scholars), we are her heirs and beneficiaries from that endeavor.

There is little doubt that sometimes Jane Austen, who never married, must have struggled with less than a "competence." She lived with her parents when she wasn't assisting a brother and his family with household and child-minding tasks. She visited wealthy friends and relatives, but she had little money of her own, even from the publication of her works. Although the first edition of *Pride and Prejudice* sold out and two more editions were published during her lifetime, she had sold her interest in the book for a mere £110. So, although Austen's works became popular during her lifetime, her own earnings from them hardly made her rich. Her whole life long, she tailored her spending to what she had on hand. In short, she practiced principles of thrift, and she wrote those principles into her characters.

Historically, the idea of thrift is connected with savings and good management, as we might expect, but it is also intimately tied with the notion of thriving, from which the word is derived. Sensible people of the nineteenth century would have connected the concept of thrift with prosperity, good fortune, and success. Thus, where modern readers might be tempted to think of thrift as giving things up or being frugal, for Austen and her heroines, *thrift* and *thrive* would have been conjoined. Acting prudently and tending to one's daily plans and expenses are not limiting acts but decisions that provide for greater benefits in the future.

Austen's novels feature both thrifty and spendthrift characters. The most likable characters are usually those who care for themselves and others through moderation. Charlotte Lucas of *Pride and Prejudice*, although we don't necessarily love her husband, is the model of a prudent housewife. Through her careful planning, her home becomes her castle—and Mr. Collins is often ejected beyond the moat into his little garden or sent up to his study to work on his sermons and snoop on the neighbors.

Compare her with the younger Bennet daughters. Lydia and Kitty, of course, are utterly improvident in what they do. And even if Lydia can see how to make good her poor purchases, her impulsive spending and wild ways provide a glimpse of her bankrupt future. Kitty may grow up and improve her character with Lydia gone from the house, perhaps even marry, but Mary is so self-centered, we can't imagine her setting up her own household or being other than a dependent of easygoing Jane and Charles Bingley (on the plus side, at least she'd scare away the even more irritating Caroline Bingley!).

We have more hope for Catherine Morland. She is a joyous, energetic character, who is also trained to thrifty living from the first we see her. Her mother has common sense and good health, and living in a large family has given Catherine considerable freedom, but she has also had the excellent household management of her mother to emulate. When the Allens invite her to vacation with them in Bath, her mother advises her to keep track of her money while she is there and gives her an account book for the purpose. Her father gives her ten guineas, a relatively generous amount of spending money, but not so generous as to offer Catherine infinite pleasure without having to watch her pennies; he promises to send her more money when she needs it. Although Catherine is a little immature in her understanding of the world, her ideas of thrift have been carefully cultivated in a happy family.

What about Emma? Emma has more than enough money to meet her needs, a house over which she presides as mistress and hostess, and the prospect of freedom to choose to marry or to remain single. Although like Catherine she is immature emotionally, she is very provident with her time and money. She takes up with Harriet Smith, a young woman of lesser means, and mentors her, although rather selfishly. She attends to the needs of the poor, bringing provisions and advice to the families under her care. What she does not do is give the example of conspicuous consumption and pride that we see in characters we like a lot less, characters like Fanny Dashwood of *Sense and Sensibility* or the Bingley sisters of *Pride and Prejudice*. She is the kind of woman that Mr. Knightley finds attractive, because she will know how to care for and conserve his estate.

Harriet Smith, Emma's young friend whose origins are uncertain, has considerably less money to work with, and she is saving of what she has. Although her taste is certainly not on a level with Emma's, she spends a great deal of time mulling over every purchase. Perhaps savoring the decision-making process is a part of her thrift; it helps her enjoy the shopping experience. Even Mrs. Smith of *Persuasion*, one of the most impoverished of Austen's characters, does her best within her straitened means. Her wealth has been utterly reduced through the actions of a scoundrel who led her husband into poor investments (a Bernie Madoff). Crippled with complications of rheumatic fever, she has come to Bath in hopes of getting better. In spite of the fact that she is burdened with her terrible difficulties, Mrs. Smith learns to be useful. She learns to knit and to work projects that can be sold to benefit those poorer than she is. In the lowest possible condition of life, through her thrifty use of her time and circumstance, she thrives. This, Austen tells us through Anne Elliot, is "the choicest gift of Heaven."

We can learn from all of these characters, and more important, we all can benefit from Jane Austen's habits and attitude and those of her most sensible characters. Living the thrifty life opens wide opportunities to enjoy the world. What could be a happier prospect than living within one's income and never having to juggle bills or dread the day the mortgage or rent is due? What could be a greater benefit than creating habits that lead to savings and security for the future? What could lead to a better future than practicing a thrifty lifestyle that becomes entertaining in itself, getting rid of the frantic desire to accumulate trendy possessions and replacing it with a new sense of values?

It doesn't make any difference whether you are like Mrs. Smith and your prospects have been reduced through the actions of someone else, or whether you are just starting out like Charlotte Lucas. In today's economy, you probably find yourself asking, like Sir Walter Elliot in *Persuasion*, "Can we retrench?" The spirit in which you answer that question can make you as happy as you determine to be. This is the moment when you can embrace your inner Jane and find a new way of life in thrift.

Anne Elliot understands the ins and outs of living within an income, even if her father and sister never will. Her mother had been a woman of "method, moderation, and economy," so the family lived within its income during her lifetime. However, left to his own devices, Sir Walter tends to live from fancy to fancy, redecorating, going to Tattersall's to gamble, acting on his impulses without a thought to the future, and certainly not paying his bills. Anne's sister Elizabeth thinks the way to retrench is through slighting her sister and acting less charitably. Anne and her friend Lady Russell come up with a plan, a plan that offers freedom from debt in as short a time as possible consistent with family comfort. All it requires is a little trimming of expenditure here and there and a greater attention to savings.

This is the same kind of method, moderation, and economy we can practice ourselves. And it does begin with a plan. The beauty of a plan is that it opens us to new experiences, new opportunities, because we are no longer operating on autopilot. Living the Jane Austen lifestyle does not mean pinching pennies so severely that all the pleasures of shopping are lost. Instead, it means finding more happiness by determining to spend wisely and live more. Maybe our weakness in the past has been entertainment. We've spent more than we should on movies or concerts when we should have been paying attention to our credit card balance. The good news is that we can follow Jane Austen's example and create *new* and thrifty ways of entertaining ourselves.

We can also have fun in planning out new ways to go about

furnishing our homes and our wardrobes. Check out any new furniture store and you are likely to discover that the furniture available is very expensive in relation to its quality. Looking for gently used options in the style that suits you can give you the endless pleasure of decision making without impulsively spending money. And we can discover classic, well-made, beautiful clothes at first-rate bargains by looking at consignment shops and thrift stores. We can keep our wardrobes fit for use by mending and amending the items that we can't live without.

Adopting patterns of thrift as practiced by your favorite Austen characters will alter your life. You will gain a new sense of pride in your ability to plan and invest in your destiny, and you will feel more confidence every day. At first, making a plan and sticking with it may mean some restructuring of your habits. You may have to trade your daily latte for a weekly treat, and then turn the money you save into an investment in yourself and your future.

We begin this book with Jane Austen's philosophy on life. All of us can gain both happiness and self-respect by living within our income and creating a personal lifestyle that includes both paying off our bills and saving for the future, having what we want and sharing with others. Then, in the following chapter, we guide you on investing and saving, as learned by Lucy Steele. Lucy was known by all as the character most likely to succeed; true, we may not wish to emulate the morality of her methods, but we have to admire the principles that lead to good stewardship of money and time. Then in Chapter 3, Charlotte Lucas is our guide to a thrifty household, whether we have family responsibilities or are on our own. She has a lot to tell us about living on a budget and thriving.

Look to Chapter 4 for help in comparison shopping; Jane Austen's thriftiest characters will guide you to the very best deals for your money. Haven't found just the right thing when you're shopping? Chapter 5 guides you to ways to transform your fashion finds, and Chapter 6 will help you avoid waste and create new fashions and accessories, tailored to your own taste.

What's a lifestyle without health and looks? In Chapter 7, our Jane Austen heroines will reveal the best and most natural ways to maintain a healthy glow on a budget. In Chapter 8, your healthy interest in life will overflow into the elegance of your environment, and with Elinor Dashwood as role model, you'll find tips for every room in your house or apartment.

Chapter 9 guides you to special occasions and places for thrifty bargains: antique sales, auctions, estate sales, and flea markets. The secrets of these events and how to bargain your way to the best price are there for you to find.

Next, we share Catherine Morland's secrets of being a thrifty traveler, whether you visit friends or relatives or seek adventure on your own. Become a gracious guest and a savvy traveler through the tips you'll find in this chapter. Travel costs money, but not all of life's pleasures do—in Chapter 11, we share some excellent advice on finding joy in life's least expensive pleasures, and Aunt Norris recommends her best strategies for finding freebies!

Look to Chapter 12 for advice on celebrating—Austen's favorite ladies and gentlemen guide us to the perfect joys of holidays, weddings, and feasts, occasions of special delight. We can have our cake and eat it, too—thriftily—with advice from this chapter. In Chapter 13, you will be reminded that sharing is a part of the thrifty lifestyle, too, so look to Miss Bates's giving spirit for inspiration as you discover ways to maintain a healthy balance in your economy. And in Chapter 14, you'll learn from Austen's characters the best (and worst) approaches to giving and receiving presents. Last, in Chapter 15, we invite you to share in the full life that thrifty living opens for you.

Just like Jane Austen, who found joy in a life lived within her means, you can have it all. So in her spirit, using the characters in her novels we've come to love (and even those we loathe, whose mistakes we can learn from), we will help you to achieve the same joy and, ultimately, to lead a richer life.

Chapter 1

SELF-RESPECT AND OTHER BENEFITS OF LIVING WITHIN OUR MEANS

*"I must live within my income,
or I shall be miserable"*

Austen very much promotes the principle of living within our means, out of respect for others and ourselves. More than once, our lovely Jane provides readers with examples of what happens when one dares to live beyond one's means. For example, in *Persuasion*, Sir Walter goes into debt after his prudent wife's death. His equally prudent daughter Anne wants him to slash his spending with "indifference for everything but justice and equity," but his impulse to buy and his desire to look the part of a landed gentleman without scrimping lead him to the brink of ruin. Then, in *Pride and Prejudice*, most of the Bennets' problems stem from habitually maxing out their income. Most of us can relate to these characters, as we probably have at one point or another acted like Sir Walter and given in to impulse spending. Or maybe we have behaved like the Bennets and pretended to have deeper pockets than we really do.

Indeed, we may recognize the pitfalls of living right up to our income, or even beyond. It could be a Starbucks habit we can't quit, or we can't say no to our friends when they are organizing a group to go to a trendy bistro for brunch or dinner. Perhaps what looked like a bargain vacation that couldn't be turned down now sits on the credit card as an unpaid balance, accumulating interest. Or maybe there was an incredible opportunity to buy a special dress for an event, and well, it was a little more than what we imagined spending. Perhaps we are living paycheck to paycheck because we are paying off student loans.

Turn to your favorite author and life coach, Jane Austen, for help. Before you can fully retrench and wrap your mind around the strategy of planning, budgeting, and saving, you must first understand the Jane Austen philosophy. Our Jane considers living within our means, without harming others, as a basic ingredient of a well-lived life. And the beauty of achieving financial virtue is that it will also prevent much unpleasantness and produce many benefits. When honorable people follow through on their promises, whether financial or personal, they can face themselves in the mirror and smile. When you and I live the thrifty Austen lifestyle, we can rest easy, knowing that we have the means to pay our bills today and face anything we may encounter tomorrow.

In studying Jane Austen, we see that we can avert many evils by living within our income, from dreading phone calls about overdue bills to being shunned by our friends for failing to repay our debts. For Austen, not paying one's creditors is the same thing as stealing. For example, if Sir Walter would not reach a gloved hand through a shop window to snatch a jewel-studded mirror or a jar of Gowland's face cream, neither should he steal by refusing to pay for the many luxuries he bought on credit to flaunt his importance as a fashionable baronet. And today, as in the Regency, one could end up in jail for debt, such as by refusing to pay numerous parking tickets and ignoring the court summons, as *Pride and Prejudice*'s Wickham would likely do. You can't hole up in London forever, Wickham! If you don't get dragged away to debtors' prison, you may still face the loss of your home and worldly goods. Repossession (or "repo," as it is called in popular parlance) is as alive today as it was in the nineteenth century. What a sight for your neighbors when the authorities descend on your well-appointed home and abruptly carry off your furniture, flat-screen TV, stereo system, computer, expensive watches and designer jewelry, and set of first-edition Austen novels, while everyone stares in disgust. The lifestyle you thought your position and tastes demanded was *so* not worth the humiliation. And what about the incalculable damage to your image in the community?

We hope you don't find yourself in such an extreme situation, or in the nearly as embarrassing position of being hounded at home for late or lapsed payments. Dealing with debt collectors and their relentless pursuit of payment can undermine your morale and cause you to sink in the esteem of those around you. Loss of reputation can destroy both one's professional and personal relationships. No one wants to do business of any kind with someone who has proven himself nothing less than a shyster and a cheat. And no one can respect someone who sacrifices principle to self-indulgence; existing family ties and potential marriage prospects can both be blighted by such choices. When several of Austen's worst characters exploit others to pursue indulgences they cannot afford, how justly we loathe the likes of Wickham, Willoughby, Tom Bertram, and Mr. Elliot! The Bennets and Gardiners end up footing the bill for Wickham's debts (so much for the already overextended Bennets cutting back on expenses . . .); Tom spends his father's money at the expense of his brother Edmund's future after throwing away his own; and Mr. Elliot bankrupts his "friend" Mr. Smith and leaves Mrs. Smith desperately poor in the wake of a sickly, isolated widowhood. Not very gentleman-like. In fact, we must tell all of you blackguards that from almost the first moment of reading about you, your manners, impressing us with the fullest belief of your arrogance, your conceit, and your selfish disdain of the feelings of others, were such as to form that groundwork of disapprobation on which succeeding events have built so immoveable a dislike, that you are the last men in the world whom we could ever be prevailed on to marry!

On a related subject, if you resist riotous living, you'll be less likely to find yourself tempted to marry an incompatible mate to salvage your finances. In *Sense and Sensibility*, Willoughby gets no more than he deserves in the ireful Miss Grey, but it is not what we would wish for anyone on entering the marriage state. Do anything rather than marry without affection. But, of course, we agree with Mrs. Jennings, and wish with all our souls his wife may plague his heart out! And what better punishment for Wickham than Lydia, or for Mr. Elliot (who almost ruins our beloved Anne Elliot's life) than the even more parasitic Mrs. Clay? She'll flatter him into bankruptcy one fine day.

We apologize for lapsing into an uncharacteristically vengeful spirit just now. Dear Readers, do you forgive us? We urge everyone to avoid the company of the likes of Willoughby and Wickham and to resist the temptation to go gaming, vacation at seaside resorts, buy more horses or hunting dogs, or order another suit of clothes.

Let us move on to the many blessings, including self-respect and independence, that rain down upon the fiscally responsible. There is integrity in fulfilling one's monetary obligations and paying all of one's bills. It is unethical to burden others because you bought what you couldn't pay for yourself, Mr. Elliot— you're not a charity, and have no right to turn yourself into one by tricking people into supporting you, to their ruin. Whatever bears affinity to cunning is despicable. There is shame in gaining something without giving anything in return, in undeserved prosperity built off the backs of others. We must not make anyone else suffer from our poor financial decisions, such as by forcing them into being our creditors and thus producing a domino effect of credit-based spending and financial stress. It is not the butcher's or seamstress's job to keep us in veal cutlets and silks while they starve. By contrast, virtue truly is its own reward. Following through on our commitments and earning our keep inspires self-respect. And where there is a real superiority of mind, pride will be always under good regulation, as Darcy knows. Fiscal responsibility is responsibility to our community, a way of loving our neighbor.

Self-respect goes hand in hand with self-discipline. Let's get back to money-jar values. This means we save up and buy only what we can pay for. If we're in debt, we must retrench. We face facts and take drastic measures, challenging ourselves to cut costs anywhere we can without harm to others, such as nearly every expense that is not already owed or currently necessary to our

survival. We experience a surge of excitement as every day becomes a personal challenge to our strength of purpose. For
many of us, this is simply a return to the frugal, hardworking,
self-denying, careful-budgeting, always-pay-what-you-owe
lifestyle of our parents or grandparents. Perhaps your grandparents raised their seven children and cared for their aging parents
in a tiny house with one bathroom and didn't get a car until
they had saved enough to buy it outright with cash. Your parents may have worked multiple jobs and raised you and your
siblings on powdered milk and hand-me-downs in order to provide you all with the best available education and music lessons.

Like Miss Bates, Mrs. Smith, and Austen herself, many of
our families made their small income go as far as possible and
strove to make others' lives better in the process. Buying things
one could not afford simply was not an option for honorable
people. We learn from these role models the value of self-denial,
prioritizing of purchases, and avoidance of debt as much as possible. Miss Bates has certainly earned a vacation from the stress
of caring for her mother and scraping together sustenance, but
she doesn't take one. Mrs. Smith would probably laugh outright
if we shared our desire for a kitchen renovation or a spa tub.
And so, like our role models, we embrace hardship for higher
principles. We downsize our homes, drive our junkers into the
ground, eat lots of noodles, and drink juice from frozen con-
centrate to pay off our debts, and our real friends honor us for
our integrity. Louisa Musgrove of *Persuasion* declares that we
are almost as upright as sailors, and we only know how to live.

When we pay off what we owe, we are free from bondage to
our debtors and gain the prosperity of peace of mind. We jus-
tify the trust others have placed in us. We are also no longer tied

to corporate strangers whose only interest in us is the interest earned from keeping us indebted. When we have steeled ourselves to live according to our income rather than our desires or impulses, we feel a sense of accomplishment. No more at the mercy of a fickle marketplace or our own shallow materialism, we enjoy a surge of independence. We feel pride in our power of self-control. We are not seduced by every shop display as Lydia is, nor unable to resist even the most absurd and dissatisfying purchase of an ugly hat. We will buy only the most beautiful hat in our budget and only with our own money, not Elizabeth's or Jane's. In our modern world, we refuse to be the dupe of advertisers and will be very selective in our purchases, whether coveting original editions of Austen's novels, a Regency gown for a ball, travel expenses for an Austen convention or festival, DVDs of Austen movies, or Austen paraphernalia in the form of T-shirts, mugs, handbags, hats, scarves, stationery, paperweights, bookmarks, teas, soaps, or mints. Perhaps we might even want to buy something non-Austen-related, but we can't think of anything at the moment.

In *Sense and Sensibility*, Robert Ferrars may have his own barouche, but how much does he enjoy it? Everything he has was handed to him and he's never worked a day in his life, unless you count the meticulous selection of a silver toothpick case as work! Thankfully, we are not dependent on the acquisition of the perfect toothpick case for our sense of importance; our contentment comes from within. With our fiscal maturation and growing self-restraint, we find ever greater pleasure in simplicity and minimalism and are even happy to live in a humble cottage. I wouldn't say we're excessively fond of it, but we get by and we have each other. We've redirected our energies to more important aspects of life than things, but because we spend our hard-earned money with care, our possessions are truly our own and we appreciate them more. We feel the satisfaction that comes when everything is earned, bought, and paid for (except oneself, Charlotte Lucas—don't go there!).

If people have acquired their worldly goods honorably, they have a right to the almost absurd pride they sometimes take in their stuff. We once saw a man walk up to a fancy, gleaming yellow roadster in a grocery store parking lot and admire it from a variety of angles, walking around and around it. To our amazement, he then got in and drove away—it was his own car! Young professionals who have bought their first suit with their own money have a special lilt in their step. Paying off a house is a major financial accomplishment that generally occurs in a person's mature years and that merits celebrating. Neither of us knows this feeling yet, but we congratulate those of you who do, especially if you achieved this triumph without the aid or condescension of an esteemed patroness of the likes of Lady Catherine de Bourgh. Only you know how many socks you darned, buttons you replaced, or home deep-conditions you performed to bring about this historic moment. You pierce our souls!

People admire those who deprive themselves for a higher purpose, in their financial lives as in all aspects of their lives. When one gains something through great effort over time, it makes an especially meaningful gift from the heart. We admit that it's nice of *Emma*'s Frank Churchill to give a piano to the woman he loves (though in a troublesome way), and it's nicer of Darcy to give one to his adored sister, but these are wealthy men who give from their bounty. By contrast, imagine the ingenuity that Mrs. Dashwood employs in planning gifts for her daughters for a humbler Christmas at Barton Cottage. More impressive, in *Mansfield Park* Fanny Price purchases a silver knife for her sister Betsey out of the remains of her spending money—Sir Thomas probably cuts off her allowance while she's at Portsmouth in his effort to punish her into marrying Henry Crawford. But most impressive are *Emma*'s Miss Bates and *Persuasion*'s Mrs. Smith, who give from nothing and are able to think of others despite their own hardships. Perhaps you most cherish the ruby earrings your grandmother passed on to you, which your grandfather gave her when their farm finally prospered, after they had sweated through many years of drought, flood, illness, and loss.

There is such a contrast between the glad givers and the toxic takers in Austen's fiction. Aunt Norris's grubbing a cream cheese and several other treats out of the servants at Sotherton is a fitting contrast to Mrs. Jennings's eagerness to cater to the tastes of her guests and to comfort Marianne during her romantic sorrows with every delicacy in the house. The fundamental difference between the two women is that Aunt Norris wants to use people, and Mrs. Jennings wants to enjoy their company. Aunt Norris's manipulative hints about leaving her money to the Bertram children are absurd, considering a significant amount of her money was usurped from the Bertrams in the first place (and we doubt she'll give it back in the end). Mrs. Jennings doesn't see people in terms of money, status, or how she can benefit herself. She embraces others regardless of their "level" or her own, keeping her old friends from before her rise in fortune and visiting them openly (as much as Lady Middleton may look down her nose at her mother's connections from humbler days). She may be a teaser and matchmaker, but every-thing she does is intended for others' good. She is a magnani-mous person who genuinely cares for others' welfare.

Mrs. Jennings is so sacrificial that she even risks her life to care for Marianne during her potentially infectious and even deadly fever at Cleveland, feeling a special duty to be a substi-tute mother to her in Mrs. Dashwood's absence. Both heroines Emma Woodhouse and Anne Elliot allow for the possibility that their men of choice love another and wait patiently with their beloved's happiness in mind, to see which woman he truly loves. What good is it to Aunt Norris to be debt-free, when she has used so many people along the way and ends up shunned and nearly alone by the end? She cares for no one but herself and ends up stuck with Maria in a self-imposed banishment, whereas Mrs. Jennings is surrounded by family and friends and has a life of congenial activity. If Aunt Norris had had even the simple generosity to be nice to Fanny Price, ironically, she could have mooched at two households—Thornton Lacey as well as Mans-field Park—and spent her elder years accumulating more free-bies in an atmosphere of much more bustle and interest than the dull misery of her seclusion with Maria.

We all know that happiness cannot be bought with cash or credit. Some of Austen's most contented characters, like Miss Bates and Mrs. Smith, have barely enough to survive with constant vigilance, but pay as they go and live large-souled lives. Others, like Mrs. Jennings and her daughter Charlotte Palmer, respectively, lack the fulfillment of marital companion-ship or brilliant accomplishments, but their infectious laughter and transcendent bliss bring us much comfort and delight. Dear Readers, let us not allow our characters to be at the mercy of circumstance. Let us always do our best to be people of integrity who live within our means, rain or shine. Like our beloved Mrs. Jennings and her kind, let us spread our goodwill like golden sunshine.

Chapter 2

Lucy Steele on Investments

". . . how to turn a good income into a better"

Lucy Steele is a clever trickster. As readers, we don't much admire her character, and we deplore the way she treats Elinor Dashwood. Poor Elinor—Lucy is engaged to marry Edward at the same time she is looking for a better marriage offer, but even though she knows Edward is Elinor's true love, she wants to hang on to him until someone richer comes along. However, we mustn't focus on her weaknesses but instead consider her strengths. Truth be told, Lucy has something to teach us about finance. Lucy is a woman determined to live within her income and to enlarge it as much as possible (alas, at any costs, but we wouldn't go that far).

Perhaps we shouldn't judge Lucy too harshly because she can't help her circumstances—she has limited "professional opportunities." She can marry, or she can marry. As an opportunist, she is determined to marry as advantageously as possible. Luckily for us, the world today offers women great professional opportunities, and financial independence can be ours if we're savvy with our money. If Lucy were around today, she wouldn't dream of marrying Edward. She would be too busy pursuing work in banking, finance, or investing, because she infinitely prefers using other people's money rather than her own. And the chances for advancement in that corporate environment would match her financial skills. But whatever her career path and salary, we are certain that Lucy would definitely prioritize managing her money, make smart investments, and maximize every single investment opportunity available to her. Just look at how she managed to turn a few careless compliments on Lady's Middleton's children into a luxury vacation in London.

Budgeting

With limited funds and even more limited access to more money, Lucy understands how planning reaps rewards. And a written plan of financial status is the best first approach to take when organizing your finances. Figure out your income, fixed and discretionary expenses, assets, and liabilities. In determining your net worth, you can see just how to allocate money and where it can best be spent. Have a comprehensive plan that helps you organize your expenses, and that will keep your spending in line with your income. In addition to controlling spending, one of the best aspects of a budget is that planning allows you to save, which will continue to increase your net worth and provide a cushion for the future.

If Lucy were around today, she would plan for every part of her financial future, based on a sensible allocation of her money between spending and saving. That allocation of funds, also known as a budget, is what allows one to make life decisions: whether to live alone or with a roommate, whether to spend money on lunch or brown-bag the midday meal, and a variety of other daily choices that can lead to a comfortable life. With a budget, any of us can make sensible use of our money, saving our funds toward both specific projects and future long-term goals, while tailoring all our other activities to our income and assets, not our whims.

Failing to budget may yield poor money decisions, leading to debt, which requires you to spend unnecessary money on interest when you could have paid cash. Lucy would have called that "paying off the dead horse," and with good reason. There's nothing so discouraging as making payments on a luxury item you no longer use or want.

Saving

Lucy always thought about her future, and you should, too. The good news is that through budgeting, you can deliberately set money aside for that future down payment, vacation, or retirement. Saving money can be very simple. Most experts agree that you should save no less than 10 percent of your monthly after-tax income. But we imagine that for whatever income she has, Lucy would save 20 percent. This would build a financial cushion for the future—a plush fringed cushion.

It may feel like 20 percent or even 10 percent of your monthly income is too much to save, so perhaps you can start with a small percentage and work up to a recommended amount. Saving the Jane Austen way shouldn't feel like a chore—it should be simple and feel virtuous. It could be a matter of gathering up all the loose change you have at the end of the day and allocating it to savings. Just put it in a piggy bank or a jar, and when you have accumulated enough, put it in a savings account. Another option is to remove all the $5 bills from your money at the end of each day; save this money until you have enough to make a deposit into savings. One way to make those savings mount is to pick one habit you may have and reduce your spending in that area to provide more savings. If you go to Starbucks for coffee every day before work, bring a thermos from home Monday through Thursday to save the money and make that latte a treat on Friday. If you go out to lunch several times a week, start brown-bagging your lunch. The goal is to spend less and save more.

Still more effective, use payroll deduction to deliver a set amount from each paycheck into a savings account. (You can't spend what you never have in your hands.) Although many banks are not interested in savings accounts with little money in them, credit unions often accommodate themselves to beginning investors and are friendly to small savings accounts, which, after all, may lead to more business in the long run. Make sure that you can't access your savings account easily—no debit card on that account. Once you've accumulated your savings, you're probably ready to consider how to invest some of that money to gain more.

Investing

Because we know Lucy is determined to live within her budget, we imagine she would turn her attention to maximizing the money she has through, first, whatever opportunities her employer has available. Most companies offer employees an opportunity to invest through a 401(k) plan. If this is available at your company, and particularly if the employer matches the contribution, financial experts suggest that you invest up to the amount that your employer matches. The beauty of the 401(k) contribution is that it can be made on a pretax basis, meaning you won't be taxed on the contributions and their accrued income until you begin drawing from the account. This allows you to use payroll deduction to save for the future, a relatively painless way to save because the money never comes into your hands. We can't help but think that if Lucy had a 401(k), she would make sure it left her employer's hands and would keep meticulous account of her accumulating wealth.

Lucy might also choose to open up a Traditional IRA or a Roth IRA. Again, investments into these plans allow her to make her money grow while giving her tax benefits. Because Lucy is a smart cookie, she will probably consult a financial planner (one recommended by a Fanny Dashwood type) early in her career in order to make the wisest investments possible. Any investment may lose value, so she wants to make sure that she diversifies her plans to increase her chances of a high return and decrease the prospect of loss. If she could stockpile tax-exempt bachelors in an account as well, you can be sure she would!

Credit Cards

Would Lucy have a credit card? Lucy would recognize the benefits of credit cards: the opportunity to make purchases without carrying cash or a checkbook, the accounting information that credit card companies offer, the cash back and discount options available, the ability to contest charges for items that either are not delivered or are substandard (she would contest charges often, of course), and the insurance benefits available for travel charged on the card. Perhaps you feel the same way. But it's awfully easy to go to the dark side with a credit card and use it mindlessly. You never want to charge an amount that you can't afford to pay when payment is due. A good rule of thumb is to record the amount you charge and set it aside so that you never charge more than you can possibly afford to pay off at the end of the billing cycle. If need be, write the check and subtract it from your checking account when you get home, so you're ready to pay for your purchase when the bill arrives.

Be sure not to build up a huge credit card balance on which interest accumulates for items that you simply should have saved up to buy or items bought on impulse. Pay off your balance in full whenever possible. In fact, the best way to use a credit card is to help establish your credit rating. It's a means to an end, but when you want to buy something that requires a substantial payment, for the most part, save ahead. The one exception is usually living arrangements.

Real Estate Investments

Of course, Lucy Steele really doesn't have to pay for her housing, because she is always living with (or off) other people. Most of us don't fit that situation, although many multigenerational households exist today where the rent is split simply because of the high cost of housing. When Lucy marries, her husband has already taken possession of a fine estate, and her first fiancé would have come with a rectory; either way, Lucy has her housing covered and avoids the stress of debating rental and purchase options. This frees her for more flattering of heartless snobs and their privileged brats.

When you, the modern, self-sufficient professional, have enough equity built up in savings, you may want to consider purchasing your own home. How will you decide when to rent and when to purchase? Most likely you will have to consider the housing market; how much does it cost to rent as opposed to owning one's own home? Buying a condominium or a townhouse or investing in a co-op apartment requires knowledge of the legal structures that govern each of these types of home ownership. All involve additional fees on a regular basis, fees you may not want to pay, can't avoid, and can't predict when budgeting for the future. In what way is this a better investment than renting, a situation in which the landlord repairs and maintains the property and may possibly be persuaded into additional concessions and discounted payments?

If you decide to buy a house, check out the neighborhoods where you can afford to invest your money. Look for a home that stands to appreciate over time, which means the neighborhood has to be one where other people want to live. Find a location where services such as street maintenance, streetlights, garbage collection, and water and sewer are reliable and efficient. Even if you have no children, determine the quality of local schools for resale purposes. Decide whether you can do the upkeep on a home yourself, and be sure to save money for maintenance and repairs.

When calculating the monthly cost of a new home, you also need to remember the expense of real estate taxes and insurance. Fees for closing costs and charges for initiating a mortgage will also figure in those payments, but if you are a saver and use your credit card wisely, you will take maximum advantage of a good credit rating in placing your mortgage at the best rate.

You will also have to decide whether you want to live alone or consider having a roommate, whose rent would offset the mortgage payment. You may even want to purchase investment property, where income from an attached or garage apartment will help you pay your mortgage. If you have maintenance skills or access to good maintenance help, this may be a wise investment. Picture yourself with a tool belt strapped on, smugly making repairs with the shades drawn and exulting in evading another expense.

Expanding Your Income

When you have a career, it can be very easy to convince yourself that you're above taking on additional jobs. But it's not a bad idea to think about how to best expand your income, if and when you're not satisfied with what you're making. There's no shame in taking on extra work—our parents and grandparents did it.

Why look for extra opportunities to make more money? Maybe you want to save for a big expenditure—you've dreamed of an adventure climbing in the Himalayas, or maybe just a leisurely cruise to paradise. Maybe you just don't make enough for your own sense of comfort—you're concerned that emergency situations may leave you short. Maybe you just want to have a little more disposable income than your current situation allows.

One exciting way to expand your wealth can come through hobbies you may already enjoy. Perhaps you love writing— consider the possibilities in freelance writing, writing filler for publications, or helping people compose their memoirs. Consider organizing health insurance claims and billing for people who are baffled by multiple documents and confusing medical codes. Maybe cleaning houses for you is like recreation for other people—some people get satisfaction from making order out of chaos; offer your skills to someone who desperately needs them. Maybe you're a real organizer, and you love a challenge; help other people organize their homes and offices, and make a profit out of your pleasure. Perhaps you're a real clothing stylist, and you love working with fashion; somewhere there is someone who is dying for your help in shopping for and organizing her wardrobe.

One good way to make more money may come through the use of online auctions. Many modern Lucys enjoy searching for bargains in their neighborhood and then selling their items online at a profit. Online sellers sell everything from antiques and vintage clothing to new items bought at store closeouts. Last year's treasures already discarded by one person may be this year's find for an online buyer. Lucy will wean Robert away from his toothpick habit by selling his collectible tooth-pick case online at a profit (which she will keep for herself). Of course, she'll boast that it came from Gray's in Sackville Street, London, the most exclusive of shops.

Lucy's auction investment for profit goes something like this. Lucy enjoys whiling away her Saturday morning going to garage and rummage sales. Because she likes shopping for clothes and other luxury items while keeping to a budget, she reads *Vogue*, *Town and Country*, *Architectural Digest*, and other upscale fashion and decorator magazines at the public library, or she window-shops at the mall so that she can recognize the latest trends and the best labels when she finds them in the course of her weekend.

If you pay attention to your buying and selling, you can pick up a handsome income on your investment from items that you simply enjoy acquiring. Best of all, you can meet people who will steer you to even better bargains. You can enhance your savings while being entertained and providing entertainment to your interested online buyers. Because eBay, for example, has been estimated to have more than 200 million users worldwide, whatever you have to sell will undoubtedly reach buyers interested in owning it.

You can find other options as well. For instance, you can become an Amazon.com reseller for CDs and DVDs. You can create a virtual store and sell from your own website. The modern day Lucy Steele will surely be tech-savvy enough to create

Savvy Selling

In setting up her sales persona, Lucy will remember that selling at an online auction has its own protocols. Auction houses, whether online or on the ground, take a percentage of the sale and/or a fee for their own upkeep and profits, so if an item requires a minimum bid in order for the seller to make a profit, that needs to be a part of the package. Online auctions usually require the seller to ship the item, so Lucy must be prepared to ship whatever she is selling properly packaged to avoid damage, with a way of determining that it has been delivered and signed for.

Describing what is being sold is another important aspect of the auction trade. An appropriate description of the merchandise and its condition is essential to avoid complaints and returns. Lucy will also learn the abbreviations that are common to listings—NWT for *New with Tags*, for example, or OOAK for *One of a Kind*. Imagine her toothpick case listing: *Silver Toothpick Case OOAK Exclusive from Gray's London NWT*. Well, maybe she's fudging it a little there—Robert has occasionally carried his toothpick case and used his toothpick (ew!). Online auctions usually have extensive workshops and tutorials to help sellers succeed at the auction trade.

a presence for herself on the Internet that will enhance her investments and leave her sitting pretty.

If Lucy doesn't feel much like doing the Internet, which requires constant tending, she can also make money through traditional garage sales. Lots of communities have big sales at a centralized location where for a small table rental, Lucy and others like her can display the items they have collected and resell them at a profit. Many of these benefit charities, so Lucy can maximize her investment by doing good for others while doing well for herself. Her motives? Don't worry—she doesn't mind doing good as long as she makes a pretty penny. Well, she minds, but it doesn't look well to complain about contributing to charity.

With initiative and education, with energy and attention, Lucy can build up her assets while maximizing her interests. And so can you. It all begins with planning and investing, spending wisely, and saving carefully. In the end, you have paid bills and a tidy nest egg. That's a good position for any Austen character— or for any of us!

Chapter 3

◈◈◈

Household Economy
the Charlotte Lucas Way

*"If she is half as sharp as her mother,
she is saving enough"*

Whatever made Charlotte Lucas marry Mr. Collins? Both we ourselves and Elizabeth Bennet ask that question. Charlotte seems a normal enough young woman; up to her fatal marital decision, she seems to have plenty of common sense. And yet . . . and yet . . . she decides to spend the rest of her life with HIM.

Oh, we know there is an internal kind of common sense to her decision. She doesn't want to end up as the unpaid nanny to her brothers' brats. She doesn't want to become the paid or unpaid companion to a grouchy old lady, like Lady Catherine de Bourgh, to pick a name at random. Instead, she chooses to be the mistress of her own household, with occasional attendance on Lady Catherine and full-time attendance on her husband.

She has chosen to marry a man who is beginning his clerical career. Although he has a prospect of inheritance (if Mr. Bennet doesn't live long or doesn't somehow produce a male heir), he is a hardworking man, and if he aims to please in perhaps a little too slimy a way, he still has hopes for additional parishes and greater prosperity. In the meantime, he has a good solid vicarage and a patron who actually seems to enjoy his too-obsequious attentions.

What we also know about Charlotte is that she is a woman of prudence and household thrift. Charlotte chooses marriage to a man whose career she can help advance by focusing on her own strengths and providing proper care for his congregation and for her own domain. In Elizabeth Bennet's early visit to Hunsford, we already see signs of Charlotte's clever household management in her creation of designated spaces for herself and Mr. Collins so she doesn't have to see him all the time. Out he goes into the garden that she encourages him to cultivate. Off he toddles to work on his sermon in his study, the room with the windows overlooking the road so he won't miss any possible glimpse of Lady Catherine and her daughter as they drive by. We know that Charlotte will be a domestic success. So what secrets does Charlotte Lucas Collins know that would be helpful to us today?

Stock Up

Charlotte is a planner. We can be sure that her household runs efficiently because she organizes its every detail. Starting with

Charlotte's kitchen, the heart of the home, she buys items on sale in bulk and stores them for later use; she invests sparingly in perishable items, because she produces so much of the perishable food her family needs from her own kitchen garden. We know her kitchen garden will provide the staples for her family, and she will manage its produce so nothing goes to waste. She will carefully store fall's bounty for use all winter. Apples and hard pears can be put away in a cold room, and blemished fruit will be used up first to avoid spoilage. Charlotte's root cellar provides great cold storage for parsnips, carrots, and other vegetables that will not spoil easily. Charlotte has no central heating, so keeping things cold is easy for her.

You may not have a garden to grow your favorite fruits and vegetables. And you may not have a cellar or even a pantry to store foods, but you should imitate Charlotte and stock up at your farmers' market or grocery store on onions, garlic, potatoes, and any other vegetables that are often sold in bulk and that you regularly cook with. Then find room in your home to store these, a darkened space where the temperature is cool and where you keep your produce in containers that give them a chance to breathe—a basket, netting, or even a colander. Though you may not realize it, last-minute grocery runs for these sorts of basic vegetables ultimately cause you to use more time, energy, and money than necessary. Consider what you spend on the gasoline to drive to and from the supermarket, not to mention the extra items you inevitably throw into your cart while at the store. Finally, even if you don't have your own garden and orchard, you can buy in-season fruits when they are at their best and most bountiful, and yet least expensive;

store them in your refrigerator drawers to use throughout the week.

USE IT OR LOSE IT

Charlotte preserves fruits in various ways: through making preserves, drying, or pickling, for example. These provide flavorful additions to the regular fare of everyday life, the gruel and the plain bread and crackers that might be the better for delicious homemade butter and jam. She makes jam cakes from her own preserves, and Mr. Collins, always ready for carbs and a confirmed consumer of muffins, packs them in as quickly as she can bake them.

You can still do this kind of food preservation today. If you have fruit trees, you know you often experience an embarrassment of riches, but your bounty can be turned into delectable treats for later eating or sharing with others. Jams and jellies make lovely gifts for special occasions, and many recipe books and websites provide original flavor combinations that can't be bought at the store. In all food preservation, follow directions that come with canning jars very carefully to make sure that homemade foodstuffs are safe. Jars and utensils must be sterilized to avoid contamination by bacteria, and many preserves call for sealing in a hot-water bath to eliminate the possibility of spoilage. If you don't have the materials for a hot-water bath so that your jams and jellies can be stored long term, you can store some items in the refrigerator for a shorter period of time.

We made a series of mango combinations including mango

ketchup, mango jalapeño jam, and mango raspberry preserves, all of which took advantage of the huge mango harvest in our Florida yards and the multiplicity of recipes available both in books and on the Internet. At Christmastime, we were able to share the summer harvest with friends and neighbors. A basic recipe for simple jams suitable for blueberries, raspberries, and blackberries, for example, requires cooking your fruit with sugar (three cups of fruit to two cups of sugar) and the spices of your choice—cinnamon, ginger, or cloves—until the berries are soft and the sugar dissolves. You can cook the fruit rapidly and bring it up to what is called the jellying or gelling point (about 200 degrees Fahrenheit at sea level). If you don't have a candy thermometer to check the temperature, the jellying point is reached when your jam thickens and congeals so that when you put some in a spoon and turn it vertically, more than one drop congeals together and forms a sheet hanging from the spoon. Pour into sterilized half-pint jars and refrigerate. Most preserves created this way will last at least a month in the refrigerator—but don't count on having any left at the end of the month, because people love homemade jam. Use it as a spread on toast or English muffins, or put it on top of crackers spread with cream cheese. Pair your homemade delights with a freshly made loaf of bread, and you have an irresistible combination for gift giving.

If you don't have enough fruit or time to make preserves, a simple compote or sauce will allow you to use up what you have and not see it go to waste. Chop up the fruit, add a little sugar as needed, and stir until the fruit breaks down a little and becomes juicy. You can then drizzle it over yogurt for a healthy

snack or store it in a glass container in the fridge to eat with oat-
meal for breakfast the next day.

Meal Planning

Many busy, thrifty homemakers plan their meals for a week and
do staple preparation on the weekend. This maximizes thrift
and minimizes waste. It can also be a great deal of fun. Why not
invite your friends over to spend a couple of hours socializing
while putting together all the ingredients for a lasagna that will
produce several meals? Or imagine devoting a Sunday afternoon to looking through recipe books, online recipe sites, popular magazines, and television food shows that will provide a
wide variety of new ideas to keep lunches and suppers exciting.

A wise old homemaker once told us that householders who
buy a whole chicken instead of chicken parts, fried chicken, or
fast food will have more nutrition for the purchase price plus
more flexibility. Imagine Charlotte savoring the decision of
whether she will have fricasseed chicken, chicken with dumplings, chicken croquettes, or whatever she can imaginatively
create from what is at hand. You can do the same: start with a
raw chicken and roast it yourself for even greater savings. Your
imagination is the limit for using all the meat that a chicken
offers—using it to create chicken quesadillas for an easy dinner,
or for lunches by making one-serving casseroles from leftovers
and freezing them in lidded glass containers. And like our frugal Charlotte, you throw away almost nothing.

Charlotte undoubtedly has her own poultry, but when she
buys butcher's meat, she doesn't have a supermarket for selec-

tion. She has to order and buy with care from her local provisioner to make sure she receives the best and most economical cut possible for her investment. For modern homemakers, buying in the grocery store when meat is on sale and freezing it for preparation later is an economical choice. If you are freezing a lot of meat, you may wish to invest in a vacuum device to pull the air out of your packages before freezing. This will help protect against freezer burn, which reduces the quality and palatability of the stored food. For foods that you will freeze for shorter periods of time, use freezer paper, aluminum foil, or plastic bags; ground meat needs to be used as quickly as possible, no more than three months after you freeze it. Check online charts for the optimum amount of time that you can maintain quality in frozen meats. Always label what you freeze and date it so that you can rotate your stored food to maintain quality.

When buying meat, pay attention to such health factors as the amount of fat in the cut. Pot roasts and stews turn tougher meat into delectable treats. Long and slow cooking can make a

Mind the Meat

In selecting meat as a protein resource, always keep in mind health issues. Don't leave meat at room temperature, but refrigerate or freeze it right away. Thaw frozen meat in the refrigerator, not on the counter. Always wash your hands when handling raw meat, and carefully wash all utensils that have touched it. Scrub counters where raw meats, even when packaged, have been sitting; consider devoting one cutting board to meat handling so that you can sterilize it after each use.

healthier meal of a less expensive, leaner cut. If only, on the same principle, a long and slow marriage to a clod could make a smarter, more discerning husband, then Charlotte Lucas would be fixed for life.

Planning ahead allows for use of one major food item over several days. No wonder Miss Bates becomes almost apoplectic with thanks over the leg of pork sent to the Bates household from Hartfield: it represents roast pork, and salt pork, and fried pork, and sausages, days and days of eating pleasure in a home where pennies and halfpennies really count.

SLOW COOKING

Charlotte would have had a modest amount of household help in the form of servants, but we have our electronic servants as well. One of the best of these is the slow cooker. You can find a slow cooker for a reasonable price at a discount store like Target or Walmart, or avoid paying retail and find a used one at a garage sale or online. Slow cookers not only prepare food with a minimum outlay of electricity, but they allow you to make substantial amounts of nutritious and delicious foods that you can package individually for lunches for the week ahead. Where Charlotte revels in the rich fragrance of chicken roasting on a spit, or stewed hen simmering in rich stock at her kitchen fire, filling the parsonage with sweet anticipation while she sends Mr. Collins out on his third walk of the day, we can prepare a delicious chicken in a slow cooker with aromas and herbal essences to suit our own tastes or those of the family: forty-clove garlic chicken, lemon chicken, and an endless combination of other flavors. For meat eaters and vegetarians alike, chili made in the slow cooker using vegetables and beans with rice or pasta will extend your basic recipe and provide a meal that's even better heated up the next day.

Suppose that Charlotte, like many of us, wants to cut down on the amount of meat her family consumes. The slow cooker also provides a lot of options for risotto-like dishes, various forms of dal and Indian legumes, lentil or chickpea specialties with bright Latino or Middle Eastern flavors, and all kinds of vegetarian meals that make some of us forget that we even eat meat. Tofu recipes also abound for the slow cooker, providing soy protein that can be flavored to the tastes of the cook and her

Little Cooks

Homemakers with children (or olive branches) can include them in the process of food preparation. A little patience yields future imaginative chefs and helpers. Children who help make menu decisions and participate in food preparation tend to be more creative in what they agree to eat, making a win-win situation for families—better and more nutritious meals can be prepared with greater thrift, and there will be little waste.

One of our friends raised four children by making a menu plan and purchasing all the major components of her family's food once a month. She would shop in between times for dairy products and vegetables as required, but she didn't purchase packaged or prepared cookies or snacks for her children. Hers snacked on fruit, nuts, and raisins, and they knew better than to demand sugary cereals or empty-calorie products advertised on television. Her family grew up to be healthy achievers with, in addition, a healthy respect for good food and thrifty living.

family. Would Mr. Collins, a trencherman and meat eater if we ever saw one, eat tofu? Only if Lady Catherine recommended it.

FAST FOOD

Sometimes, despite the best intentions, you'll have a day or week where meals just weren't planned. If and when this should arise, you shouldn't feel that your options are limited to frozen pizza or packaged dinners. They are likely to have more sodium and fat than you want to eat, and they tend to be heavy on filler such as bread, pasta, rice, or potatoes, and low on protein and

Taking Stock

Suggestions for making stock from your roasted chicken: Take the leftover bones, skin, and scraps of meat from when you carved the chicken and put them in a pot with a couple of onions, garlic to your taste (two or three cloves), a carrot or two, several celery stalks and leaves, and your favorite spices and herbs for chicken: rosemary, bay leaves, sage, thyme, parsley, or what you like best. Pull the bones apart so that they fit into your pot, cover them with water to a depth of about an inch over the top of your chicken, and cook on top of the stove over low heat for four to six hours. This should be a gentle cooking process (which can also be performed in your slow cooker). When the stock is reduced, strain through a sieve or colander. You can freeze it or use it right away in other recipes. Some people use the veggies and chicken meat from the stock to make a soup, but usually they will have had the flavor cooked out of them. Be sure to remove bay leaves and discard them after cooking.

healthy vegetables. Food magazines today feature multiple uses for readily available roasted chickens from the grocery store. The meat can be eaten as roast chicken one night, and the remainder can become sandwiches for the next day, or it can be used to make chicken and dumplings or stir-fry with vegetables. Tip: The bones and meat scraps can be boiled down to make delicious stock. With your homemade broth, you can create a third meal by adding veggies for soup or making a creamy sauce with it, adding leftover meat, and topping it with crust or mashed potatoes for a pot pie; add a salad and bread or biscuits, and you'll pat yourself on the back.

Take advantage of such products as chicken breasts frozen in portioned sizes to prepare meals on a day-to-day basis, if putting together a week's foods in advance is not practical for you. For main courses, what Charlotte would have known and what many moderns overlook is that prepared foods cost a good deal more than preparing foods because we are paying for the labor, packaging, advertising, and transportation of products that may contain too much salt as well as preservatives that we don't want to feed our families.

Take the number of pieces of chicken you need from the resealable package, and you can turn them into an endless selection of meals. Cook the breast plain and use it as meat in a big tossed salad with oil-and-balsamic-vinegar dressing. Smother your chicken breast with fresh mushrooms, peppers, and onions, add tomato slices on top, and sprinkle oregano and shredded Parmesan cheese over everything for an Italian treat. Whip up a tandoori marinade with yogurt, garlic, fresh ginger, curry spices, and lemon juice, and let the chicken breasts soak in it for an hour before cooking on the grill or in your toaster oven.

Tired of chicken? You can add a fiesta to your diet with readily available canned and seasoned black beans. Make beans and rice for a Caribbean treat—cook up an onion until it's softened, add tomatoes and beans, and mix with rice for an easy and hearty vegetarian meal. A can or two of beans can create last-minute veggie burritos: cook two cups of rice (or use one of the convenient microwave options available today). In a frying pan, sauté a diced onion with several cloves of garlic until your onion is soft. Add a drained can of beans and Mexican spices (to taste). Cook until warmed through, and then add your rice. Season with chopped fresh cilantro and lime juice. Put your bean filling into taco shells; add the toppings you love, such as avocado or guacamole, shredded cheese, and sour cream. It's an easy, quick meal that's healthy and relatively inexpensive.

Farmers' Markets

If you have a farmers' market in your area (and Charlotte Lucas would have lived near a market town where she could have shopped), take advantage of the opportunity to shop for fresh local food, an environmentally beneficial decision. Local farmers often bring their produce and even such products as meat and goat cheese to farmers' markets, where they often sell at an advantageous price. Many organic farmers retail their farm products at a farmers' market, giving you the bonus of shopping local and organic.

Just as if you were going to the supermarket, plan what items you would be interested in buying. Better yet, think of possible meals for the week and consider what items from the farmers' market would make these better and healthier, considering that locally grown foods are fresher and more often picked at the peak of their ripeness. Then, walk around the market before you make your buying decisions; this will give you an idea of what's available and what's most cost-effective.

Make friends with the local farmers. They can tell you what they will be bringing in from their gardens from week to week, and you can plan your weekly menus accordingly. Some small farms sell shares in their crops; for a small investment, you can receive a portion of what is ripe each week of the growing season. You can pick up your produce at the farmers' market, or some of these farms will even deliver it to you.

Some of the farms that bring food to the farmers' market also have pick-your-own options. Consider making a day trip to the farm to pick your own vegetables and fruit, getting exactly the tomatoes, or corn, or apples, or blueberries that you want. This will often save you money as well.

Enjoy the opportunity to purchase local honey, and talk to the beekeeper about the benefits of honey in your diet and your beauty regimen. Check out the dried fruits that some farms make available—mangoes and tomatoes locally grown and locally dried. Try the local goat cheese or goat milk fudge— you'll get hooked on them.

The farmers' market gives you an opportunity to eat locally and think globally—enjoy the satisfaction of eating fresh food while lessening the carbon footprint of your everyday life.

Grocery Stores

If you don't have a farmers' market handy on a regular basis, or if your farmers' markets are seasonal, you'll probably be shopping at the local grocery store. The trick to shopping wisely at the grocery store is never to go when you're hungry, and always bring a shopping list to keep yourself on track. Before you go, check the specials to see if they will fit into your meal plans for the future—grocery stores often have loss leaders to bring you to the store, so take advantage of them. If something you use regularly, like lean ground beef or boneless chicken breasts, is on sale, by all means stock up and freeze serving-sized or recipe-sized portions for future use.

Many smart shoppers swear by coupons. However, if you use the coupons to buy items you don't ordinarily purchase or don't need, you won't really be saving money, no matter how cheap the item is. Coupons usually apply to prepared foods, so if you've determined to do more food preparation yourself, you're better off watching store pricing online or in the papers before you shop.

Don't get fooled by "specials" that aren't really very special. These are basically items that are marked "special" but are being offered at the regular or even an elevated price. Don't get fooled by the "buy one, get one" offer if you won't use more than one of something, or if it's something you don't usually use in your cooking. For your health, do most of your shopping around the outside of the store, where you will find the produce, dairy, and meat; don't get fooled by endcap specials, and don't buy prepared foods you really don't need. If you can't find the fresh vegetables you want or if they are priced too high, check the frozen vegetables. Frozen vegetables are processed immediately after they are picked and usually at the height of the season, and they are often a better bargain than fresh, especially out-of-season vegetables that have been picked unripe and transported. Always read labels of frozen foods to check for additives. If country of origin is important to you in your buying, ask where the produce is grown, if there is not a sign to tell you.

Some grocery stores like Whole Foods offer educational programs about buying and using organic produce or shopping economically. Take advantage of the opportunity to learn more about good shopping practices. Many stores like Trader Joe's offer recipes and good suggestions on their websites—use all the free tips and recipe suggestions you can get. They will help you budget wisely for your food needs.

Investigate the possibility of food cooperatives in your area. In co-ops, groups of people become members and share the savings involved in buying staple items and produce in bulk. This is particularly cost-effective if your meal planning involves a family or a group of people.

Club Stores and Dollar Stores

Consider the possibility of becoming a member of a warehouse or club system store. Sam's Club, BJ's, and Costco, for example, offer the opportunity for "members" to appreciate considerable discounts in return for their membership fee. The range of goods offered in the club stores varies widely from foodstuffs to furniture, the clubs themselves vary from regional to international, and the membership fees vary widely as well.

Which thrifty shoppers will probably gain the most from club store shopping? The jolly Musgrove family with their many children would probably find the warehouse store a real boon because of the excellent prices on food in bulk. Storing large amounts of foodstuffs in the larder would mean a savings for a large family. For smaller families like the Collinses, with only a couple and one child on the way, the savings might not be so great—couples, singles, and small families might want to monitor the prices at local grocery and discount stores to determine whether the investment in a membership would be repaid in the number of items purchased over the course of a year.

Charlotte would probably pass on the warehouse store—no point in buying a gross of muffins only to find they are too much of a temptation for her husband. Still, with some clubs offering discounts on necessities such as gasoline, the warehouse/club store is worthy of consideration by any thrifty Jane.

Dollar stores are another popular place to find discount goods. However, the probability of the foodstuffs offered being name brand or high quality is lessened by the very low prices. If you are determined to make purchases at the dollar store, check them carefully. Would you be better off putting your money into a higher-quality item from another venue? Do you really need the item? Be aware that some wares sold for a dollar at dollar stores cost less than a dollar at regular grocers.

Cleaning

Everyone's daily living involves more than food preparation. It involves making a space where real comfort abounds—the laughter and appreciation of family and friends, the beauty created by fulfilling your own vision of the good life. And if cleanliness is next to godliness, and you're Charlotte Lucas, you have your work cut out for you. How does Charlotte Lucas accomplish all she has to do in the course of a day? We're quite sure she's a planner throughout all her daily and weekly routines.

Cleaning can be accomplished by deciding the amount of clutter one can tolerate and drawing a line there. Both decluttering and cleaning are best mastered when kept on a schedule. Charlotte Lucas would certainly have scheduled her cleaning to emphasize both important areas of sanitation—kitchen and bathroom—and regular attention to other details during the week and month. Plan a cleaning rotation through the house or apartment. Ideally, dust each room or space once a week, and polish furniture once a month. Create a calendar and keep track of the tasks that need to be done each day—check them off as they are completed. The bonus—cleaning is exercise! Make it part of a healthy living plan.

FLOORS AND FURNITURE

What you use on your floor depends very much on what kind of floor you have. Glazed ceramic tile and linoleum can be scrubbed with vinegar and water. Consider one of the various methods available. The sponge mop tends to spread dirty water around and doesn't seem to get the floor as clean. New steam mops will sanitize the floor without adding chemicals, but they may not leave a wonderful shine behind, and some have cloth pads that have to be laundered. Floor-cleaning machines will both clean the floor and leave it shiny, but they have to be stored and they often represent a substantial investment. Choose the method that works best for you.

Other flooring—wood, travertine, carpet, flagstone, slate— has different cleaning needs. Be sure to look at the manufacturer's or installer's recommendations to provide the proper care in cleaning. Using the right materials will extend the life of your floor while ensuring that it always looks its best. Vacuum weekly, or more often if you have pets.

Polish wood furnishings and paneling with beeswax or any natural oil, such as lemon or almond (smells nice, too). No aerosols. Gleaming woodwork, furniture, and accents have a rich quality and make a room look more vintage-formal and refined. We know it's tedious work, but it's really rewarding to look around a clean and fragrant room.

BEDROOMS

You probably spend a lot more time in your bedroom than you think. After all, if you're trying to maintain a healthy personal-care system, you'll get eight hours of sleep a night. Beyond that, maybe your bedroom is an oasis where you read or study. Perhaps you take therapeutic naps in your bedroom. Maybe your home office is a part of your bedroom, although that might distract from your sleeping. With all the time you spend there, it's important to keep your bedroom clean and uncluttered. When you change clothes after work or at any time during the day, hang up clothing that's not ready for laundering. Don't leave clothing hanging around. Put your shoes on a shoe rack in the closet. Make sure everything in the bedroom gives you a sense of peace and comfort, not clutter and confusion.

Change your sheets and launder weekly; always wash full loads of laundry if you can for cost-effectiveness, and wherever possible use a cold-water wash. If you can hang your laundry out to dry, you'll save considerable money on electricity as well as being ecologically friendly.

When you bring clean laundry into the bedroom, put it away right away. Try to dust the bedroom at least once a week. Make sure that the bedroom can be darkened for optimum sleep health—consider a television-free bedroom to lower the light level at night and lower your light stress level as you sleep. Sleep gurus suggest that you use your bedroom only for sleeping, but if you live in a small apartment, that's probably not possible. Instead, keep your bedroom area tidy, and make sure it's as dark and quiet as possible when it's time to sleep. No phone, no radio, just peaceful silence—cleaning the light and noise out of your life when you're ready to sleep will reap health benefits.

KITCHEN

As we've said, the kitchen is one of the most important rooms to keep clean and sanitary. However, you don't need to buy brand-name cleansers to keep the kitchen clean, so don't judge cleaning products by how much they cost. Prices at the supermarket include the cost of advertising and endorsements, things that improve the prospects of your buying a product but don't improve its effectiveness.

Instead, consider the use of basics such as vinegar or ammonia for regular cleaning (but not both together). Whenever possible, use natural products such as white distilled vinegar as an effective cleaning agent (but check to make sure any surface you are cleaning doesn't have special cleaning-material require-ments). Vinegar can be used undiluted for floors and other areas that need the extra power; for window cleaning, dilute vinegar 50/50 with water. White vinegar right out of the bottle is a fine cleaner for your countertops—its acidity takes care of most of the pesky problems such as germs and mold that you might encounter. For a scrubbing powder, mix a little dishwasher detergent with baking soda, then add sufficient vinegar to make a paste. Nuke your wet dish sponge regularly in the microwave to destroy bacteria—studies have shown this is a cheap, effective way of sanitizing your sponge.

Some more wonderful uses for vinegar? When cleaning the microwave, put a clear glass microwaveable bowl with a 50/50 solution of white distilled vinegar and water in the microwave. Run the microwave until the solution comes to a boil (put a wooden Popsicle stick or other nonmetallic rod in the bowl to avoid superheating). This will loosen the grease and spills in the microwave so they can easily be wiped away. If you're troubled by ants, spray white distilled vinegar wherever you see them coming in.

Police your refrigerator and freezer on a regular basis. Place baking soda in your refrigerator to keep it sweet-smelling. Also, label what you put in your refrigerator so you'll know when it's time to eliminate outdated dairy, produce, and meat products. Plan your menus to use up what you have, but if you haven't, get rid of outdated food. Don't keep it, thinking that you'll find a way to make good your purchase. And plan better next time—if you don't particularly like broccoli, it doesn't make any sense to buy it on sale only to have it rot. Invest in the foods you like and will eat.

BATHROOMS

Bathrooms are an important cleaning focus because they are likely to be havens for germs. They are also havens for clutter. Use white distilled vinegar for cleaning floors, tubs, sinks, and toilets, unless the manufacturer's or installer's directions call for special cleaning (such as for plastic tubs). Be sure the bathroom is cleaned at least once a week, and more often if you or members of your household are ill.

Keep the bathroom picked up. Don't allow wet or dirty towels to litter the floor; make sure there are hooks or racks for hanging up towels. If there is a dirty clothes hamper in the bathroom, make sure it is emptied so that there is no excuse for throwing things on top of it or on the floor.

Keep beauty items in order; using baskets or shelf units to organize the items you need for daily personal care will keep things from accumulating on the edge of the sink or on the counter. Encourage a policy that whoever washes his or her hair or shaves over the sink cleans it after each use; there's nothing less appealing than hair in the sink, unless it's a ring around the tub. Have each bather make sure the tub is shiny and clean for the next use.

Following a regular routine of cleaning and keeping order in the rooms you use the most provides an economical, yet effective way to create a comfortable living environment—a real home.

Daily Declutter

All clutter can be kept at bay if it never has a chance to accumulate. That means making sure all the junk mail gets sorted and discarded rather than left to reproduce on the dining room table or elsewhere. Training yourself or family members to put clothing away or in the laundry after a change means no going through the house picking up items thrown off along the way. Prompt recycling eliminates unsightly buildup of newspapers and magazines; after all, few of us go back to read that sermon again, no matter how much we esteem the parson's insight. If you think you're going to want it, clip it and put it in a binder.

Do the best you can to maintain a clean, tidy home, recognizing that some household tasks are more critical than others. Maybe you won't vacuum the living room every day, but be

Keeping Things Good as New

Washing or fixing things is generally cheaper than replacing them. Launder your bedspread at a Laundromat (they have megamachines; don't damage yours with hulking items). A slightly worn or faded quilt can look charmingly homey, so repair the frayed corner; don't rush out and buy a new one that would look glaring by comparison and clash with the wallpaper. Reglue the splitting arm of the rocking chair, stitch up the ripped place on the side of the upholstered sofa, and touch-up the scratched spot on the wall with a bit of paint. Occasionally buy new accent pillows—it costs less than replacing the whole living room set and is surprisingly effective in giving fading furnishings a face lift. But know when it's time to replace a piece—the parsonage is not the place for ugly, mismatched leftovers from your college dorm. Your furniture should be both nice-looking and comfortable.

sure to clean the kitchen counters every time you prepare food and absolutely every time Mr. Collins touches them.

Maintaining the Home

Charlotte keeps a home that is "neat and comfortable." In every respect her taste is excellent and her furniture both suitable for her house and in proportion to it. Her household has a pleasant rhythm to it, a rhythm that is welcoming to guests and inhabitants alike. And although she is under constant scrutiny from Lady Catherine de Bourgh, she is able to withstand her critiques with good grace because Charlotte knows she's an excellent manager, and she knows that Lady Catherine knows it, too.

Indeed, Mrs. Bennet pays her the supreme compliment when she assumes that Charlotte will be competent as a helpmate to Mr. Collins, as repulsive as he is. "They will take care not to outrun their income," she remarks. No matter how many young "olive branches" are added to Charlotte's household, her thrifty management will provide for her family.

We can be Charlotte Lucas Collins (minus Mr. C., thank heavens) by planning ahead as she does. We can budget our resources as well as set aside savings for the future. Like Charlotte, we can make the best of any situation and, through cheerful, patient thrift, create a household in which we and all the company around us will thrive.

Chapter 4

❧

COMPARISON SHOPPING FOR CLOTHES WITH ANNE ELLIOT AND FRIENDS

"We have been to the cheap shop,
and very cheap we found it"

Imagine you live on a tight budget in a country village in Jane Austen's age and you need to go shopping. You might have to wait several weeks for a carriage ride to town and then face a bumpy journey in unpleasant weather. If you are a woman, you must be accompanied and therefore must recruit a companion and coordinate both of your schedules with the availability of transportation. You will be grateful if a better-off friend like Lady Russell invites you to share her carriage on her planned excursion, and you will travel at her convenience (and along the way, you'll have to put up with her unsolicited advice on your love life). Be prepared for loved ones in the country to pounce at the chance to make you shop for them while you're in town. Under these conditions and with limited time and money, you soldier forth on your shopping quest armed with a carefully strategized plan of attack. This is no casual trip to the mall!

We would certainly choose Anne Elliot as our companion to help us navigate today's complex world of budget-conscious clothes shopping. Remember that Lady Russell consults with Anne alone, not Sir Walter or Elizabeth, when drafting a precisely calculated plan of economy to eliminate the Elliots' debt. With Anne's high sense of honor, we suspect she makes many personal sacrifices to offset her father's and older sister's selfish spendthrift ways and knows how to shun extravagance while maintaining the neatness and elegance of appearance that is not only expected of a woman of her class, but also a natural part of her refined sensibility. These are the skills we need in our own shopping quest.

Where would economical heroines like Anne Elliot shop for clothes today? Like respectable women of the nineteenth century, today's women have both a practical and an idealistic side. We value health, safety, cleanliness, utility, longevity, and a good price when considering any kind of purchase. But we're also elegant ladies who seek comfort and beauty that lend a grace and charm to our lives. The key is to weigh the worth and significance of the purchase against the cost. How permanent is the investment and how particular are your expectations of the desired item? When it comes to fashion, a gold locket will be worn a woman's whole life and then passed down to a loved one. A pair of gloves will wear out eventually. Hat trimmings will change as styles change and are easily replaced. But whether we're in search of something high-end or mundane, comparison shopping will make us informed buyers who know our options.

A Lesson from Jane

Jane Austen was a clever shopper who hunted down the best bargains for herself and her family. She fulfilled commissions for others with special care, sharing details of her buying triumphs and rarer failures in letters. The Austens were not impulse buyers—they shunned both unnecessary expense and false economy. Then, as now, the challenge was to get the highest quality for the lowest possible price within one's budget. Jane shopped for such things as tea, gloves, stockings, fabric, jewelry, shoes, and hat decorations, often buying for Cassandra as well. She knew that if something seemed like too good a bargain, it probably was: "We have been to the cheap shop, and very cheap we found it. . . ." One had to know where to buy what, considering the importance, price range, and risk involved in the purchase. The Austens bought their tea from the respected Twinings company—shady vendors added manure to the tea they sold. That's right: *manure*. Apparently, the Austens did not appreciate its subtle flavor and considered it worth spending more at a reputable company to avoid this distinctive brew. Jane sometimes wishes she'd paid less for an item but weighs the quality in the exchange: "I do not boast of any bargains, but think both the sarsenet and dimity good of their sort." On another occasion, she reports to Cassandra, "I have bought your locket, but was obliged to give 18s. for it, which must be rather more than you intended. It is neat and plain, set in gold." But she's very pleased with her four-shilling gloves and enjoys imagining that "everybody at Chawton will be hoping and predicting that they cannot be good for anything, and their worth certainly remains to be proved; but I think they look very well."

Where is the balance between price and quality? What items in one's wardrobe should one buy new, and what can one buy secondhand? What are the best stores for specific new and used clothes and accessories? How do we avoid ending up clad in an overpriced but shoddy-looking dress, serving tea that a sly merchant doctored with manure? Will our guests ever forgive us for either of these errors in consumer judgment?

Strategize Your Purchases

A few years ago, Charles Fishman's book *The Wal-Mart Effect* suggested that manufacturers who deal with large discount retailers might have to lower the quality of the materials in their goods as well as move manufacturing to countries where wage and safety considerations for workers are not adequate. As thrifty shoppers, we need to make sure, insofar as we are able, that the goods we buy are of high quality and will last with wear. Poor quality is a bad bargain wherever we buy it. As responsible shoppers, we also want to be assured that our purchases are not made at the expense of the safety and environmental degradation of someone else. Anne Elliot, Jane Bennet, and Fanny Price would certainly never harm others to indulge themselves, and we don't want to become callous like Fanny Dashwood, willing to trample others underfoot to get luxuries we don't need.

We once heard a financial commentator discuss the idea of amortizing your wardrobe over the period of time it will be worn. Buying fewer high-quality but relatively expensive pieces that will last and look good for ten years is more economical in the long run than buying many cheap, trendy, and poorly made garments. If I buy a classic Ralph Lauren shirt in a Ralph Lauren store or an upmarket department store and I pay $95 for it, and if I am still wearing it ten or even twenty years later (at which time it still looks good in spite of being worn and washed many times), what am I spending a year for the garment? $9.50 for ten years, or $4.75 for twenty? If I buy a trendy shirt at a discount store for $19.95 and it's trashed—doesn't wash well, doesn't hold up with wear—at the end of the year, I've wasted my money.

That's not to say that high-quality goods can't be bought at discount stores—the buyer has to take care that the quality of

A Lady Need not Explain

Buy the following items new, for sanitary reasons:

Swimsuits

Underwear

Socks

Shoes (generally)

Personal-care products, such as soap, lotion, shampoo, cosmetics

All of these items can be purchased on sale or clearance. Swimsuits go on sale at the end of the summer, and underwear can often be found on sale at outlet stores or at big annual sales. Simply plan ahead and wait as calmly as Anne Elliot would for the discounted price.

the materials and the manufacture meet the same standards as the same brand in an upscale store. As economical, self-disciplined ladies like Anne, we plan our expenditures carefully; we look at fashion magazines or articles in the papers or online and make decisions about purchases based on our real needs—for work, for leisure, for household chores—and thus keep our buying thrifty. We strategize our shopping journey with these needs in mind and consider which among the department and discount stores, outlet malls, and thrift and consignment shops in our area might best answer our purposes.

Get Creative

With Anne's cleverness, patience, and genteel taste at our disposal, we venture forth, shopping list in hand. Be creative in your comparison shopping to ferret out the best deal. If you have a small, delicate frame like Anne or small feet, for example, you may be able to get less expensive items such as shirts and shoes as well as bulk packages of socks from the girls' department (and if you have a younger sister like Margaret Dashwood whose feet are the same size, you can share). A girls' extra-large poncho in an irresistible rainbow pattern could be a perfect fit for both your personality and your physique and something you simply couldn't find in the women's department. Sometimes men's goods are priced lower than women's as well, so white T-shirts, a belt, a scarf, or even jeans from the men's department or in a larger size from the boys' department might suit you just fine. Be wary of merchants packaging things like scarves as "men's" or "women's" (or for that matter, "boys'" or "girls'") when it doesn't matter—you'll expand your selection and thus the possibility of finding a great deal.

We are going to sound like our mothers here, but don't skimp on shoes. Buy good-quality ones with arch supports that will promote a healthy posture and cushion the impact of walking on hard surfaces—daily living is an athletic event in itself. Your legs will thank you. But buy them on sale and pay attention to which stores carry the brands that fit your feet so you can get the lowest price. You may be able to find the same shoes much cheaper at a department store than at a store that sells that brand exclusively. Buy them, like clothes, at the end of the season when they are on clearance. This is the way to get well-made boots at a substantial discount.

In general, avoid buying shoes used. They mold to the foot shape of the wearer, and worn insoles and treads can cause leg and foot problems. And as proper ladies, we won't even mention the words *bacteria* or *fungus*. But if you find new-looking shoes that fit you at a thrift store or sale, go for it. We've all had false Cinderella moments and bought shoes that seemed to fit at the store but betrayed us on a first wearing thereafter.

Outlet Malls

An interesting destination on a bargain-hunting expedition is the outlet mall. In Austen's day, mall shopping probably would have been associated with shops located around the Pall Mall, a very upscale kind of shopping indeed. Remember that Colonel Brandon brings word of Willoughby's perfidy from the stationery shop in the Pall Mall, where he has overheard two young women talking about Willoughby's engagement to Miss Grey. Harding, Howell, & Co., the first department store in London, was located at 89 Pall Mall, and other upscale shops were in the area to meet the needs of the well-to-do. By Austen's day, shopping had become a favorite pastime for ladies of leisure in the city, and we can imagine Mrs. Jennings and the Dashwood sisters shopping in Bond Street, pausing to look at the unimaginable bounty on display: feathered bonnets in the latest fashion, Italian gloves in every imaginable shade, gorgeous silks to satisfy the most fastidious tastes. Mrs. Jennings could marry off a sow dressed in all that glamour.

Today's outlet malls are not particularly glamorous, but they are a big business enterprise. They bring together in one location shops selling some of the priciest brands in the marketplace, such as Ralph Lauren and Dooney & Bourke. Outlet malls feature designer clothing and personal accessories that Anne may be able to convince her snobby sister will suit her just as well as the Dior gown and complete set of Louis Vuitton handbags and luggage she had intended to rack up on Sir Walter's maxed-out credit card.

Outlet malls represent destination shopping—many require travel because they were built on less expensive, rural property. As in every other shopping venture, let the buyer beware. The origin of the discount shopping outlet was the selling of overruns, seconds, or damaged goods to employees, then to local shoppers at a discounted price. Those early mill stores in places like New Bedford, Massachusetts, allowed manufacturers to clear inventory easily and without the expense of shipping. In recent years, with much manufacturing being done offshore, the goods being sold in outlet malls may be made expressly for those venues and thus be of a cheaper quality, or they may not be current stock and styles.

The big criticism of outlet malls is in the pricing. The reference pricing (the comparison with prices elsewhere, or the "originally sold at" pricing) is often highly imaginative; the goods marked with those prices never sold anywhere at that price. Some of the goods being sold really never did sell anywhere else—they were made to be sold at the outlet mall, so there can be no comparison—except that some details such as reinforced buttonholes, quality buttons and trim, and seam finishing may be inferior in items found at the outlet mall. Some items may be left over from two seasons ago. Also, some brands, particularly those that depend on exclusivity to maintain their high prices, are usually not represented in outlet malls. They don't want to be too accessible to the marketplace for fear of lessening their market appeal. Don't forget that Mr. Elliot's unfortunate first wife supposedly married him for love but didn't look closely enough at his finishes of character to realize the inferior piece of work she was getting.

On the other hand, those who love shopping will find that a day at the discount mall can be fun and thrifty. Anne would invite Charlotte Palmer to accompany her, Elizabeth, and Mrs. Clay there, anticipating that her good-humored enthusiasm would offset Elizabeth's snootiness and Mrs. Clay's insincerity. Mrs. Palmer buys Mr. Palmer's Y-fronts at Jockey for the best price ever (while Elizabeth looks the other way in disgust), and Anne politely helps her pick the most sensible of the boys' outfits with matching accessories at Gymboree, so she can show off little Thomas on her next trip to London. All three ladies purchase a hip scarf for fall at The Gap, Charlotte laughing merrily all the while. They wrap up their trip at a jewelry outlet, where, despite Anne's best efforts, Elizabeth insists on selecting a gold bracelet etched with her monogram, while Charlotte selects an emerald ring, claiming Mr. Palmer would be quite disappointed if she did not. Mrs. Clay compliments everything and Elizabeth buys her a second-rate bangle.

Preparing for your trip by checking the kinds of items you want and the prices ordinarily charged for them will definitely repay your time and enable you to give others good advice as well—there's no bargain in something that is both out of style and of lesser quality. But there are bargains to be had for those who watch their pennies carefully.

Outlet malls can be good places to buy:

- staples such as cotton turtlenecks

- special-occasion outfits

- business suits

- designer accessories such as handbags and dress shoes

- casual dressy items such as fancy jeans to wear with heels

Discount Stores

Finding bargains at today's discount stores is one way to exercise thrift while locating the things one wants, new and affordably priced. However, as with outlets, even shopping at discount stores requires some savvy preparation on the part of the shopper—

decide what you want, compare advertised prices, and make sure the quality of the items you buy is the quality you want.

Anne would invite Harriet Smith to join her on a tour of discount stores, knowing her limited budget and how she loves to examine everything. Harriet has to be frugal about her purchases, so each one requires strategizing. She hesitates and looks, gets distracted and looks again. Harriet, grazing through a store, may be an interesting companion, more patient and willing to empathize with our own indecisions and conflicting buying impulses, not to mention the fact that her price range complements ours better than Emma's. And how Harriet would love the range of discount stores available to today's thrifty shopper! Anne can always help her to refocus and make decisions if she wanders too far off course.

Going to discount stores like T.J.Maxx, Ross, and Marshalls gives the thrifty shopper an opportunity to look over a wide variety of manufacturers and styles, to handle and try on the garments, and to take advantage of discounts and markdowns on internationally known manufacturers. Picture Lydia Bennet's delight at rack after rack of markdowns, each one guaranteed to capture the rapture of a soldier. These discount stores buy the same goods that are bought by department stores, but they buy the surplus at a considerably discounted price. Because they don't advertise the specific brands they sell, they can offer well-known and expensive brands—the same items that the department stores are selling—for discounts of 60 to 70 percent. The catch is that new shipments come in weekly, and one week the shopper may find absolutely nothing of interest, whereas the next week the store will be filled with the items she needs.

Discount stores are particularly good places to shop for seasonal fashions and distinctive styles on a budget. Always scan the clearance section first. At Burlington Coat Factory you may find a beautiful, floor-length winter dress coat for $15 that is on clearance and has one button missing. Well worth the purchase of new buttons. Because discount stores often buy from so many sources, there is more variety than can be obtained in any single retail store. Harriet Smith would go wild and need tactful Anne to restrain her from buying everything!

Go to discount stores for deals on items such as these:

- holiday and formal-event purses or clutches

- matching hat, scarf, and glove sets

- fall sweaters

- bras and lingerie

- trendy twists on basics, such as black dress pants with a built-in, trendy three-tiered silver chain accent at the waist or a red wraparound blouse that ties at the side

- "career" jewelry such as faux gold or pearl necklace-and-earrings sets

Secondhand Stores

For first-class bargain hunting that would have pleased the most scrupulous Austen heroine, we love a well-appointed secondhand or thrift store.

Many worthwhile nonprofit organizations raise funds through thrift stores, and there's an earth-friendliness to them. It's beautiful to find something you love and give it a home in your life instead of in a lonely landfill. Of course there's the thrill of the hunt, and the absurdly low price tag doesn't hurt, either. There are as many levels and price points of used clothing stores as there are of new.

CONSIGNMENT SHOPS

Consignment shops can be just the right venue for a special-occasion gown, designer jewelry, or a tailored wool coat, and some high-end charity boutiques sell relatively inexpensive (but nonetheless deeply discounted and often gorgeous) used name-brand and couture fashions. If the almost-bankrupt Elliots resided on Palm Beach today, for example, Anne would lure her sister to a couture consignment shop, though Elizabeth would insist on wearing a disguise and being accompanied by Mrs. Clay. There, Elizabeth can get a new-looking designer dress that makes her appear wealthy and important at a fraction of the cost, without anyone being the wiser. Alas, she won't be getting any wiser, either, but she'll look sharp for hundreds rather than thousands of dollars. Get to know the thrifts in your area and discover their strengths.

ANTIQUE SHOPS

When shopping for finer vintage or modern jewelry, antique shops and shows are a great choice. Remember Fanny Price and her amber cross in *Mansfield Park*? Find your own version of her treasure. Of course, your gold chain will be your own, not a sleazy offering from Henry Crawford, so you won't shed any tears about wearing it. There are a number of really good reasons for shopping at an antique store for jewelry. Antique dealers are not bound by current fashion, and they buy from widely diverse sources, including private individuals. They have precious metals and gemstones as well as costume jewelry, now very collectible. Their selection runs from small, conservative pieces to large and flashy ones—your taste will dictate your desires.

Most antique dealers can help you with your selection and offer you advice, as well as give you a much better price for any piece of jewelry than you would have to pay at a retail jewelry store, where the markups range from 400 to 1,000 percent. The best jewelry bargains are always found in estate and vintage jewelry handled by antique dealers. Many dealers who deal in high-end pieces will also offer layaway plans—pay the last payment and your treasure is yours to take home, without paying interest or service charges.

THRIFT SHOPS

Consignment and charity thrift shops alike often carry interesting one-of-a-kind items, and they aren't always expensive. Well-run midrange charity thrift boutiques often sell surprisingly nice clothing and accessories plucked from last year's closet by well-off donors. A modern-day Mrs. Jennings and Charlotte Palmer would wander about such shops joking and giggling (especially when Mrs. Jennings recognizes some of her own gowns) while the modern-day Lady Middleton, clad in dark sunglasses, awaits them in the elegant solitude of a running sedan. And, of course, Lucy Steele somehow persuades Mrs. Jennings to buy her a tailored linen dress for $10. We've discovered new, still-tagged items selling at used prices—a stunning velvet opera cape from a high-end department store and multiple pairs of brand-name women's shoes, still in their boxes (Caroline Bingley must have gone on a shopping frenzy and then never worn some of the twenty pairs she bought after Darcy's rejection). Thrift boutiques have brought us such diverse treasures as a lovely green evening gown with matching wrap for a shocking $12 (which would have been less at a basic thrift store, if it could have been found there, but much more at a consignment shop), and an astounding giant rat costume for Halloween . . . but perhaps the less said about *that*, the better.

We love that most of the secondhand shops in our area support charities, such as church social service programs, Hospice, Goodwill, the Salvation Army, and animal rescue organizations. Whenever we buy something there, it's a good feeling to know that we are helping others. Two of Jane Austen's most generous characters are themselves poor—Mrs. Smith and Miss Bates—and the novelist clearly suggests that benevolence is a state of mind, a virtue that a person of any income can and should cultivate. What easier way to help others when we're on a budget than to shop at and donate to a charity thrift store? Anne Elliot would have done as much! We can also volunteer to work there ourselves, thus emulating characters like Mrs. Smith who use their talents to care for others less blessed than themselves. People who are not members of a particular church or society may join members in volunteering at their charity thrift store, because they want to make an outreach to the various programs and services the thrift supports. Charity thrift stores and boutiques present thrilling treasure hunts that benefit those in need while providing us with plenty of low-cost entertainment.

We also love that the thrift shop experience can be filled with simple pleasures and clever triumphs. You'll find a wide variety of objects to speculate about, laugh at, or admire. And whether you go on your own or with others, you'll find a strong sense of community among thrifters of all backgrounds. People chat and exchange information with total strangers at rummage sales and secondhand shops in a way they never would at a department store. In what other context are strangers so quickly comrades, as if conspiring against conspicuous consumption and the isolation of self-interestedness, in favor of a congenial bazaar?

If you were shopping in the typical department store, you would at the least be startled if even the most sane-looking stranger handed you a skirt or sweater and said, "Did you see this? I think it would look good on you." Yet this happens all the time at thrift stores, and you'll start catching yourself doing it soon enough. People bargain-bond with enthusiasm, tell tales of thrift triumphs, and admire others' finds as a compliment to their cleverness, like one big frugal family. Thus, if you happen to be standing before a floor-length mirror trying on a blazer and a hairy, potbellied greaseball sidles up to you and compliments you on the blazer, do you run, screaming, "Psycho on the loose"? No, you smile and say thanks because you know that thrift stores are different and people are often genuinely happy for their fellow thrifters who find a good deal. Of course, nothing stops you from innocently asking the greasy gentleman, "By chance, is your name John Thorpe?"

The Thrifty Community

Characters abound in the world of thrift. This fascinating cross-section of humanity may include normal, hardworking people looking for steals; bored rich people carting toy dogs; and freaky fringe people. That guy who always tries on absurdly mismatched combinations proudly models them throughout the store, sometimes even stopping to ask your opinion of his new look. Fortunately, he never pauses long enough for you to formulate one of Elinor Dashwood's polite lies. And then there's the Mary Musgrove thrifter who insists on following close behind you as you work through racks of clothes, as if she's sure there's a great find wherever you happen to be standing. One also sometimes encounters "master thrifters" who have an almost mystical ability to glean from the slop heap the most precious pearls. Whoever one meets, thrifting broadens one's community, creating unique opportunities to trade tips, share knowledge, and affirm each other's economical lifestyle. And there's enough juicy gossip to satisfy both Mrs. Bennet and Mrs. Smith.

A Lesson from Jane

Always examine both new and used goods carefully before buying. Even careful shopper Jane Austen herself confessed to being duped into getting a damaged veil, which was intended as a gift from her and her sister to a relative: "I had no difficulty in getting a muslin veil for half a guinea, and not much more in discovering afterwards that the muslin was thick, dirty, and ragged, and therefore would by no means do for a united gift." On the other hand, sometimes, flawed favorites are worth the bargain price. A $4 vintage dress in your best shade of blue is worth the salvage attempt of experimental laundering or stitching up. Just know what you're getting and that not all such restoration efforts are successful. How much are you willing to bet you can make that dress look like new?

You must brace yourself for the excitement of "basic"-level thrift stores, which generally price most of their clothing at $3 to $15, and some even have $1 racks! Now you're talking thrift! It's handy to pick up fun, screened T-shirts for working out, or jeans for casual wear, or even a few loud and crazy Christmas sweaters to wear to theme parties. Though raised in wealth and gentility, our Anne Elliot values honorable, simple living over luxury and enjoys the company of the Harvilles over that of her own family. We can easily see her at a Goodwill or Salvation Army store with the Harville children, helping them pick out gifts for their parents and outfits to wear to the Musgroves' Christmas at the Great House. But she'll never persuade her sister Mary to step in the door!

In short, be sure you go to the "cheap shop" on your thrifty shopping expedition—one occasionally unearths gold from the dust heap. Watch out for Mrs. Clay, who would not be above winding her stealthy arm in front of you to snatch a bargain from a shelf, or even reaching into your cart while you're not looking. Of course, everyone should get work duds for painting and yard work from the cheapest thrifts (your clothes *will* get paint on them—don't play the "I'll be careful" game). Casual basics such as sweaters or a raincoat can sometimes be found for a pittance. The glory of it is, it's difficult to experience buyer's remorse when one has spent $3 on an item instead of $30 or $300. If it doesn't work out, at least one had a thrift adventure almost as thrilling as sailing on the *Laconia*, but without any danger!

If you're feeling both thrifty and daring, try a dollar-a-pound warehouse, such as the one operated by Goodwill in certain cities. It's located in an industrial part of town, and on a blustery day, one may feel inspired to roll up one's sleeves and dig in the deep bins on wheels that are lined up in rows throughout the store. Every so often, employees wheel out a picked-over bin and wheel in another containing "new" merchandise. Shoppers circle the incoming bins like vultures and walk alongside as the workers wheel the clothes onto the floor. Particularly eager shoppers with a penchant for shoes may shock decorous sensibilities by snatching pair after pair from an incoming bin and hurling them over their heads to gather up later. Customers have to dig deeper and longer to find nice things than they would at regular thrift shops, and damaged and dirty goods are always an issue. (Those allergic to dust should skip the dollar-a-pounds altogether—Anne is too delicate for this venture.) But when the final purchases are rung up, the price is ridiculously low and the satisfaction outrageously high! At these prices, even the Dashwood sisters and their mother could have dressed magnificently on five hundred a year, if they dug through the bins long enough.

On the other hand, don't waste time at bottom-rung junk shops where you don't see a single thing you want in any category at any price. One attempt is enough. If you feel like entering the store is itself a health hazard, follow your instincts. We have never gone back to the dimly lit warehouse stuffed with second-hand from floor to ceiling that somehow had not one item that could bear scrutiny in the clear light of day. These are thrift "dead zones," which have an odor of mildew, gym bag, and old campsite and a fluorescent, dusty haze in the air. Exit quickly and find Catherine Morland and the Tilneys for a refreshing walk in the countryside and a lecture from Henry on the picturesque.

Be aware that like retail stores, many secondhand shops have clearance or half-price racks as well as senior discount days and color or category sales (clothes with yellow tags are 50 percent off or shoes and handbags are 20 percent off, for example). We have been known to keep our eyes on some items, waiting until they are marked down to buy them. The risk and suspense of this game can be exciting, but, of course, if you love something at a charity thrift, buy it when you see it and remember that you're helping someone.

Thrift stores are often an excellent source of the following:

- jeans, shirts, and sweatshirts for everyday wear

- funky costume jewelry

- wool blazers

- vintage fashion scarves

- overcoats

- floor-length faux velvet dresses in black or jewel tones

Buying Direct

People often sell their own goods at garage, tag, or yard sales, through the Internet, or in newspaper ads. In general, people who take good care of themselves and their homes have probably taken good care of whatever you're considering buying, so it's less likely to harbor serious flaws. Yes, we hate to shock our readers, but it is perfectly acceptable to judge the seller secretly when considering buying something used from him or her. Of course, we realize that appearances can deceive—Mr. Elliot is especially good at concealing his taints of character. But even our Jane often enjoyed satirically judging old and new acquaintance from the relative privacy of her letters, and we suspect that there's much truth in her comical portraits. When shopping for items sold by individuals, many's the time we have quietly assessed a person to decide whether a purchase is a good risk. Here are some scenarios that demonstrate how sizing up your seller should influence your buying decisions.

A beautiful Persian area rug in your living room colors is listed for sale, and you and a friend go to see it. A clean, well-coordinated couple greets you at their tidy home and mentions that the rug has recently been professionally cleaned. Piano music plays in the background (perhaps Georgiana Darcy is visiting), and the woman holds a tea cup in her graceful hand. You bargain with the couple and they shave $50 off the price. It's a deal. Well done. You now own a stunning area rug that is sure to warm up your central living space just as you'd envisioned.

A counterexample: You stop at a garage sale and spot a pair of funky jeans in your size. As you examine them, you quickly detect a mysterious stench suffusing everything in reach. Invisible insects begin biting your ankles, and you observe a superfluity of dirty plastic junk and half-dressed baby dolls scattered in disarray on a tarp, fronting a garage filled with animal heads and rusty metal piping. The greasy character who greets you with an incoherent grunt chats with his chain-smoking friend, who scans you up and down, and then attempts a pass by way of puffing stale smoke in your direction and grinding out his cigarette into his bare palm. You crisply release the jeans, take in both boors with your flashing eyes and retort, "You are mistaken if you suppose that the mode of your behavior has affected

Dress to Impress Jane

As a true lover of Jane Austen, keep your eyes open for the following staples on every thrifty shopping journey you take:

Regency-style dress in a becoming color

Gloves

Bonnet

Ballerina-style "slippers" (dress flats) for ease of dancing

Reticule if you're not up for making your own or are too busy rereading *Persuasion* to take the time

A copy of any Austen novel

When you're decked in your complete Austenian ensemble with an illustrated copy of *Pride and Prejudice* in gloved hand, look at yourself and embrace the revelation that until this moment, you never knew yourself.

me in any other way, than as it spared me the concern I might have felt in refusing your merchandise, had you behaved in a more gentlemanlike manner." Then you march in dignified state to your car. You go, Elizabeth!

We can all be as thrifty as Charlotte Lucas and have as much fun shopping as Mrs. Palmer, but we want to avoid being as foolish as Harriet Smith might be. We don't want to buy impulsively like Lydia Bennet, on the off chance that we can create something better out of our purchase. Rather, we strive to be like such sensible heroines as Elinor Dashwood, Anne Elliot, and ultimately, just like Jane Austen herself—to find the best value for our money, and the sooner the better. But in today's retail marketplace, finding the best bargain often means that we have some research to do before we load up the carriage with our bandboxes.

When Jane Austen writes to her sister, Cassandra, "I was very lucky in my gloves," claiming she found them at the very first shop she visited, most of us shake our heads in disbelief. Although it's possible to find almost anything one could want or need at a discounted price, even the most seasoned shopper usually has to visit two or more stores in order to discover it. But with access to a broad range of shopping venues for new and used merchandise, and the resourcefulness, endurance, and impeccable taste of Anne Elliot, we shall build a wardrobe worthy of the most discriminating of ladies.

Tips:

♞ As in all thrift shopping, keep checking. There's no hard-and-fast rule regarding which stores result in the most fruitful finds, especially in the world of secondhand. Online listings by individuals or businesses may be the best option if you're searching for a specialty item such as a Regency dress for an Austen event or a ski suit for your trip to Colorado. But one is more likely to be shipped manure than to have it placed in one's hands. Exercise caution and buy only from established vendors with a known reputation for customer service (or from an individual living in the area whose wares you can examine in person with a friend). It's much easier to follow up on a problem and expect satisfaction from local merchants with a reputation to keep than from fly-by-night online sellers that may disappear as quickly as Wickham did from his debts.

❦ Don't haggle at charity thrifts. It's tacky. The one exception would be high-priced items. The price may be more flexible and the manager more willing to sell a high-ticket item to make room for more stuff. If you're not sure whether the prices are negotiable at a consignment shop, ask the manager first.

❦ Be willing to watch and wait. Compare options at miscellaneous new and used stores until you know the field. Patience is always rewarded in Austen's world. Anne gets her Wentworth; Jane gets her Bingley; Fanny gets her Edmund; and Aunt Norris gets her cream cheese.

Chapter 5

Lydia Bennet, Fashionista, and the Art of Transforming Fashion Finds

"I shall pull it to pieces . . . and see if
I can make it up any better"

Lydia Bennet bought a hat that she herself didn't think was very pretty—she says she thought she "might as well buy it as not." Later, she claims she's glad she bought it for the sake of having another bandbox, if nothing else. Her foolishness in making this purchase is a key to her character in *Pride and Prejudice*, and we think her pretty silly (as do her sisters, we suspect, when they are jammed into the carriage with Lydia's purchase). But Lydia has a plan—she will remake her hat to her satisfaction and become a fashion statement among her friends and relatives. However much she protests that it doesn't make a difference what one wears in summer, she always wants to dress to be noticed. A little addition of satin and her bonnet will be the center of attention.

Most of us are not interested in buying clothes we don't like, but occasionally we find there's something in our closet we never wear anymore and hide behind the coats. That skirt in last year's popular color is looking passé, and we have nothing that matches it. The sweater we loved so much doesn't appeal to us anymore because we don't know whether to wear it plain or accessorize it. Thrift demands that we figure out a way to make good our investment—and there are many ways of updating our look by reconsidering what we own.

Revising Your Wardrobe

In some circles, it's called "shopping in your own closet." Most of us have items in our closets we haven't really worn in a while, and it's fun to see whether new combinations will give us a fresh look and a good feeling. The separates that you bought together now appear out of date and ugly as a set. Often, there is a jacket, blouse, top, or sweater that will remake the look of a skirt or pair of pants you loved when you bought it. Things that you didn't think coordinated very well can become trendy just by recombining with other outfits you already own. Play dress-up and create new looks for yourself.

But there are more exciting options that Lydia would approve as well, knowing they would catch an officer's eye. Embellishment can create a spectacular new garment out of something you are tired of, or something that never was wonderful to begin with (maybe you were having a Lydia Bennet kind of day when you bought it!). Although too much embellishment can be too much of a good thing, a little decoration here and there can turn a ho-hum garment into something unique that will make a splash at Brighton.

A friend of ours used to embellish her denim jacket with all the awards she won when she was younger. She had a combination of Sunday School perfect attendance awards, Rainbow Girl bars, Girl Scout pins, and high school medals, which she arranged decoratively on her jacket. It looked fabulous and different, and she wore something that expressed both her personality and her achievements, and at the same time displayed an ironic sense of humor in its rather bold display of personal success. It didn't cost anything, and she created a one-of-a-kind look for herself, one that brought her compliments wherever she wore her masterwork.

A small investment in paints could transform a number of items you've relinquished to the back of your closet. Consider that pair of black ballet flats that could take on another personality with a spray of metallic gold paint on the tip. Or take that plain tote you received at a recent event and add a bright color to the straps and along the bottom. Colorblocking is always an attractive look, and now you are on your way to creating unique statements from humdrum clothes and accessories you thought you wouldn't want to use again.

Specialty craft magazines and blogs will also give you ideas and instructions that can quickly turn you into an accomplished do-it-yourselfer; oftentimes DIY involves skills that look hard but can be mastered by most with a little practice. A little inspiration, paints or metals, and the plainest outfit will express your personality in a unique and special way.

Maybe you're not a fan of showing off your past accomplishments and associations, and maybe you think adding paint to certain wares is tacky. You can still transform shirts, dresses, shoes, or anything by applying beading, appliqué, or any of a number of embellishment techniques that you can explore at your local craft stores. Maybe you or your friends own a sewing machine with machine embroidery attachments; inventing and completing your own original design to wear can be very satisfying. Some quilting and sewing shops will rent time on a machine for those who don't have access to one at home. Consider embroidering your jacket by hand with all the delicious shades of embroidery floss to choose from, or stenciling an original design decoratively on the back and sleeves. Fanny Price can banish the ho-hum white-attic blues by hanging on the wall her hand-embroidered jacket with a colorful sunset using all the shades and hues of the English countryside—what a sight to gaze upon! It restores her strength. If you don't already own a jacket, explore the possibilities at your local Goodwill: denim jackets, vests, all kinds of inexpensive outerwear offer the opportunity for you, like Lydia, to make a unique personal statement.

What's true of jackets is also true of jeans. Embellishment of jeans is a fashion that has lasted since the sixties. Yesterday's torn jeans are now being recreated with patches behind the tears to express the wearer's personality. Jeans can be brought from shabby to super chic with flashy rhinestones or Swarovski crystals for casual glamour, or they can be painted with patterns or designs. Embroidery will give the hippie look that never really goes out of style among the more bohemian. Artists apply text to their jeans to express themselves, and all kinds of metallic decoration can be added in patterns to give flash and panache to jeans you were tired of and ready to retire. Like jackets, jeans are readily available in all styles, sizes, and colors at the local thrift store, so don't feel you have to buy new ones or use your old ones—maybe you want to practice your techniques before you apply them to your favorite old jeans. For as little as a dollar and sometimes even less, you can often find just what you are looking for.

Inventive Projects

Austen's ladies would not have had garments with pockets in them as we do today. Instead, pockets were separate items, like little bags, tied around the waist with a fabric belt or a string. They were frequently worn under the petticoats, so outer garments and petticoats often had a slit in them in order that a lady might access her money without appearing indecent. Pockets were capacious enough to carry various items the lady might need, without her having to encumber her hands. Ladies often carried coins, pincushions, thimbles, handkerchiefs, penknives— in short, anything a lady might need in the course of a day and would be reluctant to ask a friend to provide. These interior pockets also helped her avoid pickpockets and cutpurses who might have been tempted to steal more readily accessible carryalls.

However, over the course of Austen's lifetime, ladies' garments became less bulky, the number of petticoats lessened, and the pocket became less practical. It was replaced with the *ridicule* or *reticule*, which was actually a bag much smaller than a pocket for carrying coins, handkerchiefs, and items for a lady's personal grooming, such as a small mirror. (Later in the nineteenth century, the separate pocket morphed into the pocket inserted and sewn into the side of a lady's skirt or jacket.) The ridicule would express a lady's personality and would match her outfit or display her ostentation. Remember the vulgar Mrs. Elton plunging her letter into her purple-and-gold ridicule, so excessive in every matter of taste. That was the letter with which she was trying to guilt Jane Fairfax about not accepting a governess position in which Jane had no interest. How very royal of Mrs. Elton to presume to queen it over others and to carry that regal ridicule.

Thrifty ladies today who don't want to carry a heavy handbag can re-create the reticule by crafting small bags to carry a credit card, change, and other items indispensible in everyday life. Simple patterns for small bags can be found on the Internet and in reprints of old needlework patterns. Paint, embroider, or embellish a reticule to match different outfits, and you will have a unique fashion statement; create your reticule by recycling fabric you love from a garment you never wear to be even more thrifty.

Check online for bloggers who share your interests to get great new ideas. *P.S.—I Made This* offers wonderful, trendy ideas for updating your wardrobe. The motto of the blog is "Reimagine, Reuse & Reinvent," so the fabulous projects you find there will help you think about new ways to rework your own outfits. *Say Yes to Hoboken* gives you great directions for recycling and updating your thrift finds, as well as the stuff you have hanging around your own closet. See CraftGossip.com for imaginative projects such as transforming adult garments into cute children's clothes or other crafty projects that will spark your own imagination. Better still, Google your way into the world of thrifty folks like yourself and find the bloggers who speak to your thrifty heart.

Exchanges and Completions

Maybe refurbishing what's in your closet doesn't appeal to you because you're really tired of your old clothes and you can't imagine, in your wildest dreams or fashion nightmares, ever wearing them again. However, they're too good to give away. Perhaps you've changed sizes, for better or for worse, and you just don't want the reminders of the past hanging around. Many thrifty ladies have solved this problem by having an exchange event, where each guest brings a number of clean, neat items that she wants to exchange and receives a credit for each item she contributes. For each item she brings, she can pick something she wants that someone else has brought. (Be sure you plan a fair way ahead of time to determine who gets first dibs on things, such as by drawing numbers, or you could have a free-for-all. Or maybe your friends will think the best part of the day is finding things they want, then negotiating with other guests for items they want more!).

Invite friends and acquaintances in all sizes and with all kinds of tastes, as many as your party space and patience will accommodate. Sort the items by size and by type of item: skirts, suits, pants, purses, shoes, or whatever the guests have brought. Make it a Jane Austen event, and have a tea party while you're all poring over the possibilities. Provide paper bags with a cute saying on them to enhance the fun—entertainment and thrift, what a combination! Not only will everyone bring home something of interest, but everyone will be talking about your event for weeks to come. You'll be a star.

Perhaps you don't want to take on a new project using one of those lonely left-behinds in your closet because you already have too many unfinished projects as it is. Remember when you started that baby quilt, and now the baby is graduating from university. Remember when you thought you'd knit scarves for all your friends for the holidays, and all you have to show for your good intentions is a bag of beautiful wool lurking underneath your pile of undone ironing in the darkest region of your laundry room cupboard. Now you're tired of everything you've started.

It's probably a well-kept guilty secret that many of your friends have similar projects hidden away. We once attended a quilt show where a lovely appliqué quilt hung with a label that said, "Begun in 1960, finished in 2008, her first and only quilt." At least that quilter finished her project. But if you are burdened by the fabulous beginnings that you can't quite bring to fruition, consider alternative thrifty possibilities.

In today's entrepreneurial marketplace, many women have started little companies that finish other people's unfinished business. If your project was really beautiful and you've just run out of steam (maybe a long time ago), you might want to turn it over to someone else and pay to have it professionally completed. This will work particularly well if you were creating something spectacular with heritage materials that you wanted to pass on to the next generation; if you were just making something from a kit that you've tired of or don't have the energy to complete, you may want to move on to a new artistic aspiration.

Consider organizing a social group to work on those guilty secrets—Finishers Anonymous. Most of us who have abandoned projects we labored over by ourselves will find new energy when we get together and craft with others. Suddenly what seemed a chore becomes a real pleasure. Set up regular meeting dates; have coffee and refreshments, and discuss your favorite Austen book as you work. Many projects really don't take that long to complete if you work on them regularly. With all that flurry of painting tables, netting purses, and covering screens, you will have what Mr. Bingley would call a truly accomplished gathering of ladies. An hour or two a week and you'll be surprised at the progress you'll make. Have a little "show" of your accomplishments periodically to boost everyone's spirits. It's a good way to connect with friends while getting things done. And if you have an attack of giggles in the course of clever conversation, Lydia and Kitty would join in wholeheartedly (in the laughter, not the cleverness).

But suppose you find that your once-entertaining project that seemed so exciting has just bogged down permanently. No matter what you do, you can't boost much enthusiasm for it. Have a project exchange—maybe your friends would like to swap their unfinished items, too. When everyone has something fresh to work on, the chances of the items being completed and not wasted (or stored in the dark) grow. Keep your new project once you're finished, or exchange it back for your own finished item. It's a win-win situation. Imagine Elinor Dashwood completing all Emma's artwork that languishes almost done, and Fanny Price picking up those dropped stitches from which Mrs. Bates must inevitably suffer because of her poor eyesight, and you've got the picture!

Suppose that none of these solutions works for you. Maybe you can't envision any way that those tired bits and pieces in your closet will ever become treasures again. Perhaps you don't want to take another stitch on that plastic canvas that your mother-in-law talked you into buying ten years ago. You look at all the shoes in your closet that you never, ever want to wear again. What's a thrifty lady like you to do?

Donations

There is always a way to get those items to someone who wants them, and that is by donating them to a local charity resale shop. Pick the charity that matches your own interests, and you won't have difficulty finding a new home for your castoffs. Make sure the items that you donate are clean and usable; if you really have worn all the use out of your shoes, throw them out. If you've discovered that you can no longer stand the way they pinch your feet, no matter how cute they are, send them on. The beauty of this kind of recycling is that you give someone who needs what you have the opportunity to have it at a thrifty price. You help an organization whose work you support and pass on clothes to those who need them. What satisfaction!

In spite of her apparent willingness to throw Anne Elliot under the proverbial bus, Mrs. Smith in *Persuasion* offers an inspiring example of a giving spirit. A virtual cripple, the woman has lost her husband, her money, and her health, but she fills her time and expends her energy helping those who are even less fortunate than herself. She has had to learn the skills she uses so that she can employ them on behalf of others.

Despite her disability, isolation, and impoverishment, Mrs. Smith transforms her leisure activities into charitable acts. She uses her talent to create thread cases, pincushions, and card racks, unnecessary items that ladies would make to exchange among themselves and their acquaintance, demonstrating their self-sacrifice, discipline, and generosity. Nurse Rooke, her landlady and companion, sells these handicrafts to wealthy women under her care, and Mrs. Smith gives the proceeds to others in worse straits than she is. As she tells Anne, these crafts "supply me with the means of doing a little good to one or two very poor families in this neighbourhood." Through selling her crafts, Mrs. Smith creates a successful small-scale charity.

You may not be able to create crafts to sell yourself, but consider what you have that you no longer need and others could use. Business clothing, for example, can be very useful to women who are learning new skills and need appropriate dress for job interviews. An old bridesmaid dress that sits in your closet could make a great prom dress or formal dress for a young lady hoping to look pretty at her next dance; check Donate MyDress.org for opportunities to share that prom experience. Consult dressforsuccess.org to donate women's business attire so that others have a better chance of dressing professionally and landing a better job. And perhaps less altruistically, you can gain a deduction for your donation on your income tax, if you ask for a receipt.

Even Lydia Bennet wasn't so silly that she wouldn't see what a great achievement that would be!

Chapter 6

❧❧❧

ELEANOR TILNEY'S CLEVER ECONOMIES

"Muslin can never be said to be wasted"

In *Northanger Abbey*, Henry Tilney holds an extraordinary conversation with Mrs. Allen and Catherine Morland in which he impresses them both with his extensive knowledge of muslin. Further, he boasts of his sister's skill in conserving her resources, using leftover scraps of material to make "a handkerchief, or a cap, or a cloak." All of this conservation rests on the choice of quality raw materials to begin with, the kind of muslin that meets with Henry's approval.

Austen and characters like Eleanor Tilney, we can be sure, were used to conserving the materials that they had at hand, removing and reusing trim and lace when they were forced to repair a sheet by cutting it in half, seaming the finished sides in the middle, and hemming and trimming the "new" sheet. When they cut down the worn sheet into pillowcases, they removed and reapplied the lace once more. When the pillowcases wore out, the lace was saved for other projects and the fabric from the pillowcases became handkerchiefs or rags or some other useful item. Often at estate sales, the remains of someone's thrift show up in collections of lace waiting for another use. Better that than the note on a lovely, pristine Belgian lace apron at one rummage sale: *Saved for a special occasion . . . that never came.* Jane Austen surely believed in living with and using the beautiful items we're fortunate to have around us.

Recycling materials from our everyday lives means that we have to be conscious from the beginning of the quality of things we buy. A low price does not necessarily signify a bargain, especially if the item is poorly made of inferior materials—if we buy items of quality on sale, our money is better invested than if we buy cheap goods at cheap prices. They will fray or wear out long before we have gotten our money's worth of satisfaction out of them. Both Mrs. Allen and Henry Tilney warn Catherine that her spotted muslin likely won't wear well.

Recycling Everyday Scraps

From the day we make our purchases, we can start thinking of ways to avoid waste and make optimal use of what we acquire. Like Eleanor Tilney, we will use every scrap. Take, for example, those of us who are short in stature and who are forced to buy jeans or slacks with legs much longer than we need. The leftover material when we cut off the legs to hem the pants can be useful to create a bag to hold either toiletries or shoes when packing a suitcase or carry-on.

The method: Take the tube produced by cutting down the pants for hemming. Turn it inside out with right sides together. Sew a seam on the raw edge where the pants have been cut. You can use a sewing machine for this, or you can simply hand-sew the seam. Turn your newly made bag inside out, and the original pant hems form a finished edge. Slip shoes or whatever else you desire into the bag for storage. The best part—you have two matching bags. Minimal sewing skills and materials are required, and slipping shoes into these bags when packing keeps other items from being soiled and spoiled. With Lady Catherine's special concern for the correct way of packing, these would surely have been items of use and interest to her.

Perhaps you aren't in need of another toiletry bag or shoe bag, and maybe you aren't eager to sew. You can always take a fabric square and repurpose it as gift wrap: Simply place a gift in the center of the square and tie up the four corners. You now have a handsome presentation.

PIECING, APPLIQUÉ, AND QUILTING

Another productive use for cherished fabrics is turning your memories of good times in a garment into quilt squares. Jane Austen pieced quilts, and you can still see one that incorporates pieces from sixty-four different kinds of fabric at the Chawton House Museum in England. We can emulate her thrift. Piecing, appliqué, and quilting projects can be small or large, plain or fancy. Piecing squares, oblongs, and triangles of fabrics together can provide a new fabric from which you can create items as large as coverlets or cut out projects as small as glasses cases. Stitching beautiful flowers in appliqué on the surface of another piece of fabric can provide beautiful and colorful accessories in an otherwise plain room.

Using the fabrics you have on hand from cast-off clothing can provide a new outfit for you or meaningful gifts for your family and friends. Perhaps Jane Bennet remembers her wedding journey by incorporating pieces from a special traveling dress into a baby quilt. Add photographs transferred on fabric or signed muslin blocks to fabrics from significant occasions, and you will have a keepsake to be cherished forever.

Learning to piece pattern blocks or apply appliqué or quilt with batting is very easy, so easy that many local communities or quilt shops have classes available to anyone from the beginner to the experienced quilter. Pieced coverlets with batting can be quilted—joined together with running stitches in geometrical patterns or decorative designs—or tied, knotting yarn or thread regularly at intervals to tie together the backing, batting, and pieced top. Television shows are devoted to piecing and quilting, and books and DVDs can offer the instructions you need for any project you want to tackle. YouTube and other online videos provide a wealth of short instructions, and the beauty of these is that you can watch them over and over. Find a local group of quilters and you have access to countless years of experience and plenty of willingness to teach and share, so your projects will benefit from others' instruction and experience.

Crazy quilting is another form of piecing that doesn't really require batting but does require imagination. Suppose, like Isabella Thorpe, you want to remember your first meeting with an attractive man by the outfit you were wearing—"I remember I wore my yellow gown." Piecing together various shapes on a foundation (like your worn sheet), you create a pattern that celebrates the memory of your special occasion through the reuse of your favorite materials. Add to that embroidery and embellishment, and you have a decorative panel that can be used as a cushion cover, as a throw for your sofa or bed, or even as a basis for a vest or skirt, for the advanced sewer. Again, television programs and library books can help with planning and design; only your imagination will hold you back from creating something beautiful and memorable out of something left over that might otherwise be wasted.

MAKING CREATIVE TOYS

If you have scraps after completing your quilting project, consider making them into dog toys for Lady Bertram's pug and catnip mice for your favorite feline, toys for the Harville and Musgrove children, or even ornaments for Christmas or other holidays that call for decorations. Use simple shapes, such as those provided by cookie cutters, to cut out your project; putting the right sides together, stitch around the outline of the shapes, leaving an unstitched opening for stuffing. Turn the toy right side out through the opening you've left; stuff it with cotton, wool, or polyester (stuffing you can buy at a craft shop or recycle from old pillows); and slip-stitch the opening shut, pushing the raw edges inside. YouTube videos, sewing books and magazines, and other Internet information sites will help you learn simple hand-sewing techniques that make this project easy and quick to complete. Remember, for toys for pets and small children, don't use any materials that could scratch or cut or that might fall off and be ingested, and avoid making toys so small that little ones might swallow them.

If you're making an ornament, put the right sides together and add the batting on one side. Stitch around the outside edge, leaving an opening for turning the ornament right side out. With your scissors, trim the batting close to the seam line to avoid bulk when you turn your ornament. When you have turned your ornament right side out, push the raw edges in and slip-stitch the opening. You may need to press the ornament with a steam iron so that it will lie flat. Embellish the outside with whatever appeals to you, such as sequins, beads, or ornamental embroidery, or alternatively quilt your ornament in a pleasing pattern. These projects provide original holiday gifts that will remind your friends and family of your imagination, ingenuity, and care for them long after the holiday is over. Picture the delight of all Nurse Rooke's patients enjoying the opportunity to acquire exclusive Mrs. Smith ornaments and toys to give to their friends.

FELTING

Are you tired of your wool sweaters or skirts? Maybe they have become pilled through use and care, or perhaps they have developed holes from wear or even from moths. Don't throw them away. They can be made into felting projects—heavier, creative, and more versatile for crafters than the flimsy commercial synthetic felt available in the stores. Although many knitters and crocheters create new items to make into felt, old sweaters and other knitted goods (and fabrics) can be felted and turned into purses, embellishments (like flowers), mittens, and soft toys, to name only a few projects. Instructions for felting can be found online as well as in many craft books. Craft programs on television may also demonstrate felting. Felting is a fun, easy project with multiple uses.

The basic principle is to take woolen fabric and treat it alternately in very hot and cold water, wringing and rubbing it energetically each time you apply the water in differing temperatures. Many felters add detergent to the hot water, just as if you were washing the item in hot water in a washing machine (another felting method sometimes inadvertently applied to wool sweaters, with unpleasantly unexpected results). Alternate between the hot and the cold half a dozen or so times, then put your item in a hot dryer or lay it flat to dry. Work with the felted fabric as you would other fabric. It will be thick enough that you will probably use hand-sewing techniques to make your project rather than a sewing machine. Simple patterns and designs are readily available online and in books, or make up your own shapes, layer them up, and stitch them together to form ornamental flowers, or whatever other project you can think up. Imagine the delight of Mr. Woodhouse when Emma wears warm, felt mittens to protect her hands on a brisk, winter walk.

Larger pieces of felt can be made into small purses by creating a long oblong, folding it up, and slip-stitching the sides. Tack a piece of yarn in a loop to one side of the top of your bag, and sew an ornamental button to the other to provide a closure. Add your felted flowers for decoration. Even Lady Catherine would admire such a project.

RUG MAKING

You can also use leftover fabrics or clothes no longer useful to you to make rugs, just as people did in Austen's day. Two common types of rugs are braided rugs and hooked rugs. Although most commonly made from woolens, they can also be made from other materials such as cotton, which will vary the weight of the finished products.

For both braided and hooked rugs, cut the raw material into strips. The width will vary according to your project; braided rugs are normally made with wider strips of 1 to 2½ inches, hooked rugs with very narrow ones, of no more than ¼ inch.

For braided rugs, sew strips of the same color or material into longer rolls; trim the fabric close to the seam line with pinking shears to avoid lumpy spots when you braid. Fold the strips to be braided so that the outer edges are folded to the center and the whole strip folded again at the center line, leaving the right side of the fabric exposed with no raw edges. Metal braiding devices that help in folding the fabric strips smoothly are available to assist in the folding, if you plan to make a lot of rugs. Braid three strips together. Lace the braids together with a strong thread or cord, coiling them in the shape you want. Traditional rugs are usually round, square, or oblong. Many rug braiders taper the strips as they end the rug so they can be secured in the least noticeable way possible.

Hooked rugs are created by pulling loops of material or even leftover yarn through a loosely woven backing such as burlap, and in England, the craft is as old as the Viking invaders. In the mid- to late nineteenth century, the rugs were often hooked on burlap sacks in which grain or potatoes had been delivered.

Hooked rugs can be made on a frame or by holding a smaller piece of fabric in the hand, or even with a sturdy quilting or embroidery hoop. Draw a design on the loosely woven fabric. Make an outline in a dark color by pulling loops of yarn and fabric from the back through to the front with a rug or crochet hook. Fill in the center by hooking loops of one color or fabric, or by combining colors in a mix that pleases your eye. Designs can range from simple geometrics to complicated scenes. When the whole base fabric is hooked, finish the edges by sewing bias tape around the outside and folding it under the rug, securing it with slip stitches. Iron-on bindings are available, too.

You can make hooked projects as small as coasters and seat cushions or as large as you can manage. Some people finish the back of the rug with a sturdy lining; other techniques call for using a latex coating to keep the strips from pulling through. For safety, use a skid-proof padding under your masterpiece. Picture the Martins sitting around a homey hooked rug in their pleasant parlor, drinking tea.

Always a Bridesmaid's Dress

What about fancier fabrics like those in those bridesmaids' dresses that are too good to throw away, but that you know you will never wear again? Dream up new treasures out of unwanted materials. One project that you can create with the children in your life is a Barbie bedroom with curtains, bedcovers, and other accessories from your beautiful bridesmaid finery—those fantastic colors that brides like to make their attendants wear never look out of place in a Barbie bedroom. And what about Barbie herself? Make whole Barbie trousseaux from just one bridesmaid's outfit. The little girls in your life will think you are wonderful.

Of course, our Barbies are intelligent, respectable dolls whose fashionable garments fully conceal their disproportionate "assets" and who spend much of their time reading Barbie-sized editions of Austen's novels and making witty conversation with Fitzwilliam Darcy Ken dolls.

That they are truly "accomplished" need not be mentioned.

PILLOWS AND SACHETS

If the color of your dress is not too garish, make pillows for your own bedroom and living room. Interior designers currently use lots of pillows on the bed and the sofa; try pricing them, even at a discount store, and you can see what a bargain your bridesmaid outfit pillows will be. You can create a simple pillow by following the instructions that come with pillow forms, or once again, go to the Internet and look at sites that give directions for projects. Embellish your pillows with buttons or embroidery, with bugle beads or sequins, according to your taste. Not only will you have tastefully recycled something that you were never going to wear again, but you now have a unique personal statement. Catherine Morland, no doubt guided in creating such tasteful decorations by Henry Tilney, will look around her home in married bliss as she remembers Eleanor's wedding to her viscount through those lovely recycled muslin pillows.

Another unique way to use your bridesmaid's dress or any other fancy fabric or lace that you may have from a garment that has gone out of style or is irreparably damaged is to create sachets that will provide a wonderful scent to your linens (sheets and pillowcases) or in your dresser drawers among your intimate garments.

Sachets are easily made. Cut simple shapes from the fabric in the size appropriate to their use. Cut smaller circles, ovals, or squares for sachets, larger ones for decorative, scented pillows. Seam the shapes with right sides together, leaving a space for turning. Turn the sachet right side out and stuff with sachet materials. Slip-stitch the opening closed. For additional decoration, before you sew, place lace around the perimeter of the shape between the right sides with its finished edge facing toward the center of the project, and when you turn your project, you will have a lace frill around the outside. Alternatively, you can apply decorative lace or other embellishments in any pattern pleasing to you after you have turned your sachet.

How will you fill your sachets? Charlotte Lucas Collins would collect and dry the petals of particularly fragrant roses from Mr. Collins's garden to put in sachets. If you receive a rose

Eleanor Tilney's Tips

Be an Eleanor Tilney and don't let things go to waste.

Create Eleanor's elegance by never discarding good materials. Eleanor would be reworking that muslin from a dress into a reticule, from a reticule into a sachet, from a sachet into a protective pad to put between her precious china dishes.

Look at the things you are considering discarding and see how they can be transformed into treasures that you and others will cherish.

bouquet with fragrant flowers, you can apply the same technique. We don't have a drying shed or dry cellar to dry the petals, so we dry them on paper plates in the living room. You can use lavender or other herbs as well. When they are dry, they make a wonderfully fragrant filling for recycled treasures. Look up potpourri recipes and add spices such as cinnamon or cloves to enhance the scent of the roses. Give sachets away as gifts or use them to create a fragrance signature.

Chapter 7

❦

A Heroine's Health and Beauty on a Budget

". . . he began to compliment her on her improved looks . . ."

Jane Austen's most beauty-conscious character is male—Sir Walter Elliot in *Persuasion*. Sir Walter is infamous for his substantial collection of mirrors, which enable him to admire himself at any time (Admiral Croft has some of them removed when he and his wife move into Kellynch). He's worse than a "model scout" of today, scanning faces in the street and once reporting the shocking statistic that not one woman in eighty-seven of his random sample was handsome. While we suspect Sir Walter's "data" is skewed, we can acknowledge that we all want to look and feel our best (and thus avoid relegation to the plain column during his next face-count!). For Austen, health and beauty go hand in hand, and neither has to be expensive.

Exercise

Essential to Jane Austen's health and beauty regimen is exercise. We know it promotes both our physical and mental well-being. So we conscientiously join gyms that charge us costly initiation and monthly fees, and then sometimes quit going out of boredom or distaste for the gym atmosphere. Fortunately, however, there are some Austen-inspired ways to stay fit and healthy, without breaking the bank.

WALKING

Walking is the most common form of exercise in Austen's novels. Of course, both the author and her characters often walked of necessity, because it was the most accessible form of travel available. However, though we have other modes of transportation, we can still gain as much benefit and pleasure from it today. When research shows that walking is the best form of exercise, because it's a simple activity that's easy on the joints and still allows us to get our cardio in, we should really consider implementing it into our daily routines. Also, Dear Readers, walking is free.

We know from famous walker Elizabeth Bennet, who treks three miles through the mud to visit her sister, that it gives Elizabeth a glow. Remember how Darcy appreciates that her "fine eyes" are brightened by the exercise. And while Caroline Bingley's invitation to wander about a room pales by comparison to Elizabeth's robust cross-country hike, we would never discourage any walking and admit that pacing a room can show the figure to great advantage. Taking 10,000 steps a day is a commonly recommended goal, though some experts encourage a more customized number that factors in one's age and starting activity level. We suspect that twenty-year-old Elizabeth walks at least 12,000 steps per day, whereas 6,000 steps may be a reasonable starting goal for the older Mr. Bennet, who rarely leaves his library. The more traditional prescription of at least thirty minutes of continuous walking three days per week is advised by many as well. To measure your steps, use an inexpensive pedometer, which you can buy at a discount department store like Target or a sporting goods store on sale.

People sometimes dismiss walking as dull, but there's an easy remedy for that. Vary your scenery by rotating locations. Even a short excursion away from home can give welcome variety to one's exercise—consider a day trip to a nearby state park, preserve, or garden that Marianne Dashwood would relish. We are all so used to doing things within a certain radius of where we work or live that we often miss opportunities to regale our thoughts with a stunning view of a quiet wood, roaring river canyon, or majestic mountain. Take inspiration from Fanny Price, Edmund Bertram, and Mary Crawford of *Mansfield Park*, who all enjoy exploring the beauties of the Sotherton estate (until the latter two abandon Fanny to a bench and go off flirting). Clearly, Fanny needs to improve her cardiovascular conditioning in order to keep up with the competition. However, it's best to increase your activity level gradually, taking rest breaks as needed to rhapsodize on the view.

Each day, you could walk in a setting that would appeal to a different Austen character (and maybe a different side of yourself). Mrs. Bennet would enjoy simply strolling through your neighborhood or friends' neighborhoods and trolling for local news and gossip, whereas Mrs. Jennings would explore the liveliest areas of your city, and on a cold winter day, the Musgrove sisters would wander the megamall with glee. If you find yourself wandering a park that has lost its charm with familiarity, just imagine you are energetic Elizabeth Bennet traversing the beautiful grounds of Pemberley or Rosings. Perhaps she has just told off Mr. Darcy and is feeling particularly refreshed!

The beauty of walking is that even when you step out of your daily routine, such as when away from home, you can still incorporate it into your day. When traveling, be sure to take advantage of intriguing places to wander. Pack an umbrella or appropriate gear to protect you from any weather you could encounter. While people other than Marianne Dashwood usually prefer to take outdoor walks during fine weather, you may want to join Marianne in the rain (just avoid rambling through copious wet leaves or stumbling down steep hillsides, as Marianne learns the hard way). Though Catherine Morland liked a tumble downhill in her youth, with maturity, she learns to enjoy civilized, adult walking.

If you pick a sunny day to go for a walk, pack some sunblock and a hat. While there's no harm in getting a little sun, you definitely don't want to burn.

HORSEBACK RIDING

Oh, to be galloping at great speed through an open field, to feel the wind in our hair and Aunt Norris at our backs . . . If we are Maria or Julia Bertram or Mary Crawford, we're bold riders who love a good gallop. If we're as delicate as Fanny Price, tamer

Happy Feet

Wear good shoes for walking. This means well-made athletic shoes with arch supports. You don't need a matching teal sweat suit with racing stripes, however. Just take a walk. People-watch, relax, observe the world around you. It doesn't have to be a race with Elizabeth to be beneficial!

horseback riding provides us with a moderate form of exercise to help build our strength for more active exertion.

But most of us also can't afford horses, or stables and upkeep, or even riding lessons, or, let's face it, the gas to drive us out to the stables for the lesson. Therefore, horseback riding is recommended only if you have wealthy friends who can and are willing to foot the bill for this hobby (and not expect anything in return, Willoughby!). Besides, it's not a good pastime if you already have too much in the way of Lydia Bennet's "high animal spirits," which need not be encouraged. Plus, your mother may send you off on horseback in the rain to nab a man, so it's a potentially dangerous activity for any respectable lady. We do not advocate catching colds as a dating strategy.

The same health benefits that horseback riding provides—strengthening of the posture-related core muscles of the back, abdomen, and pelvis and improved flexibility and coordination—can be obtained more cheaply and easily. Pilates and yoga also effectively target the core and enhance flexibility. Websites such as Groupon, LivingSocial, and Bloomspot regularly offer deals on Pilates and yoga classes. Consider taking several classes through a discount package. Once you have mastered the fundamentals

and understand the safe, correct way to do the poses and move-
ments, you can invest in a recommended video and do the exercises at home, free of charge. Crunches, reverse crunches, and
push-ups also strengthen the core muscles. Whenever you are
doing any form of exercise, correct technique is critical to avoid-
ing injury as well as maximizing the health benefits of your
exertion. We never want you to have to sit out a dance, especially if Mr. Knightley asks you (not out of charity, but because
he really really wants to dance with you).

DANCING

The ideal form of exercise for most of us is the kind we don't
know we're doing. Dancing is an excellent choice. Emma strikes
the doting Mrs. Weston as "the complete picture of grown-up
health" and "loveliness itself" while dancing, and she looks so
attractive that Mr. Knightley is inspired to confess that he loves
to look at her. As with walking about the room, dancing displays the female figure to great advantage. Several vivacious
characters love dancing, suggesting it's an especially energizing
pursuit—Lydia Bennet, Marianne Dashwood, and Henrietta
and Louisa Musgrove are all enthusiastic dancers. They all also
happen to be enthusiastic about certain men (and in Lydia's
case, about *all* men). Dancing gives Austen's female characters
the opportunity to get to know diverse partners and discover,
confirm, or question their romantic interests. It gives them per-
mission to touch a potential mate, to press hand to hand, to be
held in a kind of embrace and feel each other's proximity, to
exchange blushes and sidelong glances and bits of banter . . . to
move about the room together in different patterns as if meta-

---

A Potential Mate

Consider finding a walking or dancing partner whose witty conversation you enjoy. You must choose your dance partner with care, because you may be stuck with him for two dances or as long as an hour.

---

phorically auditioning for a life in motion together through many twists and turns. Not only that, but dancing is fun! It's a healthy, safe way to meet new people (as long as you don't run off with them). Sir William Lucas would urge you to dance, even if you dislike the amusement in general and are irritated with your proposed partner.

In short, get regular exercise, one way or another. Or mix it up and begin the day with a walk, follow up with horseback riding after tea, and conclude with an evening of dancing. Current fitness trends emphasize the importance of variety and fun in our exercise routines to help us stick with them and enhance our overall wellness, while reducing stress. Workouts that alternate between or combine elements of yoga, Pilates, boxing, spinning, dance, and cross-training elements such as "muscle confusion" activities are encouraged. Changing out our routines will likely prevent overuse injuries while keeping us motivated. Treating exercising as a social event also makes us more likely to keep it up—consider the buddy system, small-group fitness classes, or workout parties. Also incorporate as much physical activity into your daily life as you safely can. If you happen to have the misfortune to have to work for a living, side-step this inconvenience by at least dancing to and from your car.

A friend of ours deliberately parks farther away from her office and the store than necessary, to add more exercise to her day. If possible, always take the stairs rather than the elevator (but don't jump down the Cobb!), carry out your groceries rather than using a cart, rake the leaves and sweep the sidewalk for yourself, and use an old-fashioned push mower on the grass and a shovel to remove snow. After all, we don't want to end up softies on the sofa like Lady Bertram!

Skin Care

Fresh air is another health benefit of outdoor activity that is also an effective beauty treatment. Indeed, the bloom and freshness of youth can be restored by a fine wind. When Anne Elliot walks by the sea at Lyme, how pretty she looks when the ocean breezes kiss the color back into her rosy cheeks, and both Mr. Elliot and Captain Wentworth take notice! For both Anne and Elizabeth Bennet, walking out in the clean air seems to highlight their beauty like natural makeup. Sir Walter notices his daughter's improved complexion and asks what she's using, assuming it's his beloved skin cream, Gowland. But to his surprise, she uses nothing. Austen mocks Sir Walter as a product groupie (as well as a shallow person), suggesting beauty cannot be bought with fancy products. We agree. A healthy lifestyle and a simple skin-care regimen are more than sufficient to bring out our natural appeal.

For example, a jar of organic coconut oil makes an inexpensive, long-lasting, chemical-free skin moisturizer, and it smells nice, too. No need to rush out and buy Gowland. Wash your face with something mild, such as glycerin or goat's-milk soap. Witch hazel makes a cheap, effective astringent, and lemon juice works as a natural exfoliator for oily skin—look for recipes that include these ingredients online. If you have a rosemary bush in your yard, toss some sprigs into a pot of water and boil, and hold your face over the steam for a few minutes for a pore-opening facial. A rosewater spritz can be refreshing on a hot day when you don't want to rough up your delicate skin by repeatedly rubbing sweat off your face. There are many recipes for natural skin treatments in books and online; they contain wholesome ingredients such as honey, green tea, yogurt, and tomato. Always keep your skin type in mind and develop a regimen that works for you—oily skin doesn't need as much moisturizing and if your skin is very dry, you'll probably want to avoid astringent altogether. For that matter, frying or peeling your face off to grow a new one was not an option in Austen's age, but we are so bold as to declare that she would not spend her hard-earned funds on such a strange and unnecessary procedure. Stroll by the sea instead!

However, as Sir Walter knows, too much sun can damage and cause premature aging to the skin, so it is wise to limit your sun exposure. Proper hydration and sun protection are your skin's best friends. Drink plenty of water throughout the day; it helps to keep your skin moisturized and to cleanse the entire body of impurities. Do invest in a high-quality, chemical-free sunscreen with "broad spectrum" coverage. Not all sunscreens are created equal, and some do not protect skin from both UVA and UVB rays and also contain potentially unsafe ingredients. Regular application of sunscreen is important even for navy men and anyone else whose outdoor life would otherwise weather them before their time. Unlike Sir Walter, we find freckles charming, but we'd rather not be "rough and rugged to the last degree, all lines and wrinkles" and "not fit to be seen" like the unfortunate Admiral Baldwin! Women, also beware of going out in the cold, as it may cause your nose to turn red, and the sharp winds may make your skin grow coarse like Mary Musgrove's. Emma's father, Mr. Woodhouse, would add the caution that everyone should stay away from drafts. And poachers.

Sir Walter isn't above wanting his feet to look handsome as well. A few basic recommendations for foot care are to wash your feet daily, slough off callused skin with gentle use of pumice (don't pumice joints), apply lotion to moisturize (no lotion between toes), and apply sunscreen to bare feet at the beach. Wear cotton socks that absorb moisture and comfortable shoes. Trim nails on both hands and feet, but not too short (cut straight across so nails don't stick out beyond ends of fingers or toes and then file gently; use separate, bona fide toenail clippers on toes).

For hands, as for feet, wash with mild soap and moisturize. We also strongly advocate the return of gloves as a fashion staple. All respectable Austen heroines and heroes wear gloves daily. Of course, wear waterproof ones for dishwashing and cleaning. Wear thicker work gloves for all labor, whether indoor or outdoor, especially if it involves equipment—a shovel, rake, broom, vacuum, or mop handle repeatedly rubbing against hands can cause blisters and calluses. Wear gloves outdoors not only for warmth, but to protect hands from sun aging in all weathers. They're also a wonderful throwback fashion statement that conjures up images of Sunday Best and dressy Southern parties and fifties chic and a proper Regency lady politely grasping a dashing gentleman's too-eagerly proffered hand while chastening him into humility with the challenge of her flashing eyes.

Happy Hair

Ideally, use only safe, organic, all-natural substances on your hair as well as your skin, and choose fragrance-free whenever possible (artificial fragrances are often poorly regulated and can contain hundreds of ingredients, some of them undesirable). Avoid such ingredients as parabens, sodium lauryl (or laureth) sulfate, silicone, and petrolatum, among others. Choose shampoos made of natural oils or butters or make your own—the fewer ingredients, the better. More companies are now making healthy hair, skin, and beauty products that don't use animal testing and are nontoxic for us and the earth, which Jane Austen would approve. But research each product you're considering using before you buy it, and be aware that labels like *organic* and *natural* can be misleading—the product may contain only a small amount of either organic or natural substances. Refuse toxicity—get the Wickhams and Willoughbys out of your life. They come in a pretty package but aren't good for you.

You can also help your hair by not blow-drying or using a rough brush or dumping styling products on it. Let it be. Skip a day of shampooing occasionally. Choose a hairstyle that not only suits you but works with your hair's natural qualities and is easy to maintain yourself, without depending on gadgets and lots of product (even if it's product you're sure is safe and healthful). Consider what length and style would best flatter your facial features and proportions as well. If your face is rounder, you may want to wear your hair longer and closer against your cheeks to elongate your face, whereas if your visage is long and narrow, a shorter, fuller style may suit you best. Bangs may be a good idea on someone with a broader forehead. Experiment with your hair and discover your most flattering look. Should your hair be swept away from your face with lots of height on top, a part on the side, a bun, vintage clips, curls gone wild, or pageboy chic? Take your hair where it wants to go. You'll know when you're messing around with it or consulting with a trusted stylist and suddenly, the *wow* moment comes. You almost pity Henry Crawford for discovering too late how pretty as well as principled you are. Thankfully, you're beyond his reach.

For the cut itself, consider the following low-cost options:

- Have a hairstylist friend or family member do your hair, in exchange for your skill in another area.

- Go to your local beauty school and ask for an instructor or a senior student who is experienced with your hair type.

- Clip a discount coupon for a cut at a family salon.

- Trim your hair yourself. There will be no debate over how much to cut.

If your hair doesn't turn out perfectly every time, don't stress—it's temporary. Besides, for what do we live, but to make sport for our neighbours, and laugh at them in our turn?

Go Natural

Using a smaller amount will offset the sometimes higher cost of buying safer, more natural, higher-quality hair, skin, and beauty ingredients or products. Investigate special sales and coupons on these items as well, and be aware that good hair and beauty products and supplements are sometimes available in generic or store brands at health-food grocers like Whole Foods.

This simple approach to hair care and styling will save you money, be healthier for you and the environment, and make you look your natural best. For Austen, the high-maintenance look is out and the real you is in. Down-to-earth Elizabeth is more beautiful and fun to be around than showy narcissist Caroline Bingley any day!

Healthy Diet

Of course, a good diet is essential to Jane Austen's health and beauty plan. Together, her characters provide us with sound nutritional advice. Everyone drinks lots of tea in Austen's novels—never forget the importance of proper hydration. Drinking plenty of water will promote your overall health and make your skin clearer and your hair more silky. Likewise, consume "good fats" such as olive, coconut, and grapeseed oil and omega-3 fatty acids (found in fish and some plant and nut oils).

These good fats are also known for keeping one as mentally sharp as Elizabeth Bennet or Elinor Dashwood.

Protein's importance cannot be underestimated. Harriet speaks for walnuts, Louisa Musgrove and Captain Wentworth choose hazelnuts, and Austen herself expresses enthusiasm for fresh fowl from the hunt. Willoughby and Wickham suggest wild game, whether in animal or human female form (because they are the worst of libertines!). Mrs. Jennings sees merit in fish, fowl, or veal, while Miss Bates delights in a haunch of pork. Bingley feeds everyone white soup.

It's recommended for digestive health that you get plenty of fiber in your diet as well. Don't worry—Mr. Woodhouse will offer you many a bowl of gruel and keep you company with a bowl of his own, while keeping you safely clear of drafts and dangers well beyond your own powers of imagination. A regular helping of probiotic yogurt labeled *live and active cultures* is also known to promote digestive health. Sickly Anne de Bourgh would likely feel a lot better if she took her daily yogurt.

Farm-fresh produce is another critical ingredient of good nutrition. If Mr. Knightley invites you strawberry-picking on his land, grab a basket and go, even if Mrs. Elton is also invited. And be sure to claim some of the juicy Donwell Abbey apples before Miss Bates gets them all.

Whatever you do, go for variety. Austen praises all kinds of foods in her letters, and her characters have diverse tastes as well. Think of the rich diversity of fresh foods Harriet will enjoy in her new life as wife of a prosperous farmer: fresh eggs and dairy and seasonal produce galore (we'd be jealous if she weren't such a scatterbrain). Rotate your food choices and avoid "selective eating," a common problem among children today;

we hazard the hint that these children are not unlike the dear Middleton offspring—if we had charge of those fine boys and precious Annamaria, they'd eat their broccoli and like it!

Moderation in all things. Avoid both Dr. Grant's overindulgence in rich foods and Fannyesque fits of fasting. If you drink, take one glass of wine from Mrs. Jennings. The occasional dessert is likewise acceptable, as Elizabeth Elliot affirms when she discovers it makes a cheaper, more convenient thing to serve

Health in Your Pantry

Use spices and herbs with potential health benefits. Cinnamon may help to lower cholesterol, garlic to enhance circulation and fight cancer, turmeric to reduce inflammation, and ginger to treat nausea, for example (which comes in handy if one spends too much time in company with the Eltons).

Take Charge of Your Health

Everyone knows you should have an annual checkup. Next time you are scheduled to have yours, have your nurse practitioner or physician arrange to test your blood intermittently for vitamin and mineral deficiencies (common ones are D, B, iron, and calcium) and improvements, and adjust your supplements accordingly. This will improve your energy level, among other benefits. Also get tested for food allergies/sensitivities if you think you may be reacting to something in your diet. Oranges are not healthy for someone who is allergic to them. Perhaps poor Anne de Bourgh's real problem is that she's allergic to her mother's presence.

guests than a full meal. Robert Ferrars and Mrs. Clay enjoy their ices. But limit your sugar consumption: The Musgrove boys eat more sweets than are good for them at the Great House and go home sick and cross. And Mr. Woodhouse begs us to avoid cake at all costs.

Inner Beauty

Jane Austen encourages us to pursue intellectual and cultural activities that will enrich our lives and enhance our understanding of ourselves and others. Caroline Bingley thinks the "accomplished woman" has a certain aura of culture and grace that comes through in her air and manner of walking, the tone of her voice, her address and expressions. Mary Crawford and the Musgrove sisters play the harp largely because they know they look pretty playing it, but they miss the point. Poor "smart, stylish" Sophia Grey is rich in money but in little else and ends up unhappily married to a mercenary man. An accomplished woman is more than a mere image of elegant sophistication. For Austen, a woman's beauty stems from her brains. She uses her intelligence to deepen her knowledge and appreciation of the world. The more wisdom and insight she gains, the more she grows as a person, and thus the more attractive she becomes. Through extensive reading of great works of literature (such as Jane Austen's novels); being informed on events both past and present; attending outstanding concerts, plays, and art shows; and continually pursuing new interests, we become ever more like Austen's best heroines, who know what matters.

HAPPINESS

True happiness enhances one's health and beauty. Austen understood the interconnectedness of mental and physical health long before it was a hip topic of mainstream medical discourse. Remember how Anne Elliot gets more beautiful as she regains a sense of her own value and of hope for the future? How Marianne recovers physically and emotionally as she learns what's important in life? A life of meaningful action on behalf of others is excellent treatment for the doldrums. There is nothing like employment, active indispensable employment, for relieving sorrow, as even the subdued Fanny Price discovers. Be as attentive to your mental and emotional well-being as you are to your physical wellness. Mental health is fostered by active, virtuous living, which naturally promotes positive self-esteem, and by the pursuit of healthy, authentic, loving relationships.

True Beauty

A cynic of the present age might with reason point out that beauty is a mere question of genetics. One is born a Jane Bennet or a Mary Bennet, a Lady Bertram or an Aunt Norris. If one is Catherine Morland, one considers being described as "almost pretty" a pleasing compliment. In truth, we do not all possess the "Elliot countenance." But for Austen, attractiveness is not clinically defined. It's not about an exact size, type, or look that one should obsessively endeavor to imitate. Beauty is not only subjective but richly diverse in its manifestations. All different body types are portrayed as appealing, whether the curvaceous Harriet Smith figure or the slender Emma type (and Emma prefers Harriet's brand of beauty!). And diverse eye colors and skin tones are also given their due. When Edmund Bertram's passion for Mary Crawford transfers to Fanny Price, he quickly "learn[s] to prefer soft light eyes to sparkling dark ones." We highly doubt that our Jane slathered on a mask of heavy makeup every morning, and we're not *Cosmo* girls ourselves. Her heroines let nature be their makeup—the blush of the sea breeze and the eye-brightening spark of a brisk walk—and the milk of human kindness is their moisturizer.

Austen and her characters teach us what we already knew: that regular exercise, a nutritious diet, a moderate lifestyle, and emotional wellness lead to overall health, and when we feel better, we look better. But we also already knew that for Austen, true beauty really does come from within. Therefore, the best beauty treatment is to develop our inner beauty. We can all probably relate to our Jane's remark in a letter that "Pictures of perfection, as you know, make me sick and wicked . . ." and we may not picture ourselves spending hours of hilarity hanging out with righteous Fanny Price and sweetsy Jane Bennet. But Elizabeth Bennet, Marianne Dashwood, and Emma Woodhouse are spunky, intriguing women who become really good people as well—they show us that a virtuous woman doesn't have to be boring. From all of Austen's novels and letters we learn the same lesson about beauty, one that we're more likely to hear when it's taught with such style and wit: a beautiful person is one who leads a beautiful life. And if you are much like the revived Anne Elliot, even her father admits (though all he can see is her outward beauty) that "Certainly you cannot do better than continue as you are"!

Choose Your Challenge

The key to an effective health and beauty routine is to do what works for you. The intensity of an exercise program can be easily customized to suit your needs and changing fitness level. For example, you can add hills and small hand weights to your walking routine to make it more challenging, or cut the intensity of an interval workout by doing fewer repetitions at a slower pace.

Chapter 8

⚜

ELINOR DASHWOOD AND THE ART OF ELEGANT HOMEMAKING AND ENTERTAINING

Being "above vulgar economy"

How does one live a frugal life without losing the graces, charms, and touches that make one's home a place everyone wants to be? Elinor Dashwood quickly learns to strike this balance. She is a model of both politeness and practicality in all her dealings with family, friends, and daily living. When she and her mother and sisters are plunged from wealth into relative poverty on the death of her father, they must adjust their lifestyle without abandoning their gentility. As a newlywed on a limited budget, Mrs. Edward Ferrars will likewise need all her cleverness to be both fiscally responsible and a liberal hostess. Where can one economize and where does one have a right or even a duty to splurge? Even our beloved Jane knew that there are times to indulge in the delights of life without cutting costs, to "eat ice [sherbet] and drink French wine, and be above vulgar economy." Like Elinor, many of us face the challenge of creating a home space that beautifully reflects who we are—our tastes, personalities, and values—at minimal expense, a home that embraces all who enter it, not unlike an Austen novel does.

Furnishing and Decorating Your Home

First, we must acquire the furniture staples for each room, the anchors of Elinor-like stability around which we can build our aesthetic vision. Most of the pieces we need and want can be successfully acquired used. New goods are not always better—quality and craftsmanship have deteriorated significantly in the mass market, and poor economic conditions contribute to this trend. How many people walk into a furniture megastore today and find the new furnishings the scale of the Brighton Pavilion, but so cheaply made that they seem ready to collapse at any moment in a heap of toxic-smelling upholstery and staples? Ugliness of design abounds everywhere in all products, and one wonders if a team of Mr. Collinses competed to offer the most vulgar styles or to fawningly compliment the ideas of a boss with even worse taste. As Elizabeth would reflect with a sigh if she shopped in our current stores, "If only Mr. Darcy were in charge! His taste is neither gaudy nor uselessly fine."

The homes of cultured people, such as lovers of Jane Austen, should reflect a cozy elegance that invites them and their visitors to relax and be themselves while finding mind- and soul-expanding inspiration in their surroundings. Go for an uncluttered (but not threadbare) look that incorporates the colors, styles, textures, and overall arrangement of furnishings that you find beautiful. An attractive environment enhances our mood and sense of wellness and brings joy and vitality into our world. Creating and maintaining an aesthetically appealing home space is part of the artwork of daily living. Thrifty chic takes time and thought and creativity but not riches. Spend where it matters and scrimp where it doesn't, and revel in your romantic retreat. Even Marianne must approve. As with all thrifty shopping, when it comes to finding good buys on home décor items, the best practice is to be awake to possibilities. Scan carefully for things that suit your style, budget, and imagination (and some great accessories are probably sitting in your closet or attic [or that of someone you know] right now, ready for a new life, like a resuscitated Marianne).

THE DRAWING ROOM

The drawing room is the most important social space in your parsonage, the heart of the home where friends and family gather for tea and convivial conversation. Hold true to your quest for the real elegance of Pemberley—many beautiful gently used antique and contemporary furnishings can be found at consignment shops. When on a quest for higher-ticket items such as living room furniture, it is usually best to proceed to a boutique consignment or upscale used furniture store. Those with a large showroom enable you to consider multiple viable sofa and side chair options at one location; they are usually in good shape, in a variety of styles, and of normal human scale. Attractive area rugs are hard-to-find treasures in the second-hand world—look everywhere in thrift venues for those. You may manage to grab one at a lower-end thrift store for under a

hundred dollars, an unusually good buy even for a used manu-
factured rug, but then never see a decent one there again, and
get your authentic Persian rug for $400 through an online list-
ing. Quaint rocking chairs, on the other hand, are commonly
available at thrifts; Mrs. Dashwood would settle in and tell you
all of her latest imagined plans for the transformation of Barton
Cottage into another Norland. If she becomes a clever thrifter,
with Elinor's guidance, she can at least approach its refined
comfort.

If your taste runs to new, more modern furniture, consider
stores like the international enterprise IKEA, which offers a
wide range of furnishings at low prices. Many of their savings
are accomplished by allowing the buyer to assemble the furniture at home, thus saving on assembly and installation. IKEA
offers not only home furnishings but interior designs for kitch-
ens, including cabinets and appliances. And especially for
young homemakers on a budget, this provides a practical and
thrifty opportunity to set up housekeeping with a brand-new
sleek modern black sofa and contrasting white bookcases.

Inexpensive side tables in shapes that coordinate with your
chosen seating can be found used in many places but usually
come in singles at thrift stores. To get a matching pair, you may
need to buy them new on clearance or at an estate sale or nicer
consignment, but remember that individual orphan tables can
be painted or draped with festive fabric to better match them up
and coordinate them with your room's color scheme. Get a handsome entertainment center at a cheaper thrift like Goodwill—
keep checking until you see one in the size and style you want;
they're a common sight in thrift stores. Choose one that closes

like a wardrobe to keep your living room appearing elegantly tech-free when you're not watching the rare enlightening television program or an Austen movie—the TV is not the center of a cultured person's home.

As for the entertainment itself, buy your media system only new and at a deep discount sale—watch the ads and be willing to wait as patiently as Elinor does for Edward, and your efforts will be amply repaid. For more cultured entertainment and as a striking inspiration for musical gatherings, pianos complete the elegance of the room. You may find one at a moving or rummage sale, auction, or thrift store, or used at a music store, or a neighbor may spontaneously offer you one for free. You may pay anywhere from nothing to well over $2,000, depending on the make and model. The key question is, do you love the sound? More important, will Marianne? Get the least expensive one that is pleasing to both your ears and your eyes.

It's remarkable how striking a space can become through the right combination of elements and a color conversation that works. For example, let's imagine a hypothetical scenario in which you as a modern-day Elinor orchestrate the perfect look for a charming drawing room on a budget and thus gain inspiration for how we might transform our own. On entering the drawing room, we're immediately struck by the pretty periwinkle sofa, which contrasts nicely with the glowing gold-beige wall color and honey-maple rocking chair and also coordinates harmoniously with the crowning glory of the room: rich satiny gold-and-deeper-blue-striped drapes with a thin stripe of contrasting white that pull the color scheme together. The paintings of landscapes and of overflowing flowerpots accentuate your room colors as well as adding touches of hot pink, peach, and orchid, making them a brightening accent (and as you are smugly aware, the greater diversity and brightness of colors in the pictures works well because of their smaller concentration and more muted background tones in the space). How did you orchestrate such classy comfort on your marginal means? You already had the old couch, which you covered with the periwinkle bedspread you had stowed away after repainting the bedroom. The pièce de résistance—the dreamy drapes? You pounced on them with ill-concealed eagerness at an estate sale (even Elinor has her emphatic moments). The landscapes came from thrift stores (or as an Elinor, you may have painted the landscapes yourself, and they are considered very good of their kind!). You cleverly found the interior paint on discount in the "oops" section of the hardware store's paint department. Finally, you added your mom's bronze-toned lamp, your aunt's hand-knitted throw, and a couple of pots of African violets. Now all you need is the company of a good-natured friend like Mrs. Jennings and a glass of Bordeaux to complete the room.

THE DINING ROOM/KITCHEN

Whether you live in a studio or one-bedroom apartment by yourself, a condo with roommates, or a home of your own, your dining area needs to have a special focus and perhaps the sense of gracious charm and dignified sociability Elinor fondly remembers from her youth at Norland. A lovely wooden dining room table, with proportions to fit your available space, anchors your eating area and invites your guests to join you for lunch or dinner. If you have room, add a buffet or hutch that can double as a storage cabinet. If you can afford only a card table, brighten it with accents such as pretty placemats or a charming table-cloth and centerpiece that express your personality.

You can find a dining room table and chairs that fit the room's proportions and a china hutch or buffet at all quality and price levels in the thrift circuit, but we recommend midrange home fur-nishing consignments as a good place to start. You can identify a respectable midrange thrift store by its merchandise (little or no junk, some antiques, and fair to relatively high prices for the sec-ondhand world—but still way lower than buying new). In addi-tion, the shopkeeper has arranged the goods with some care for aesthetics, there are no scary smells, and there may be soft music playing. The environment would be acceptable to the cultured Elinor and Marianne if they were to seek affordable furnishings for new lives on a budget in a modest ranch in the 'burbs today.

Moderately priced consignment shops have well-preserved, attractive furniture and are often willing to bargain with cus-tomers. Monitor specific pieces and the longer they are in the shop, the more likely the seller will be to cut the price. Kathleen watched a gorgeous carved-wood buffet for more than a month at a consignment shop where she had purchased other items and established a relationship with the proprietor. She made her interest and maximum price known, left a phone number, and occasionally "visited" the buffet. One fine Saturday, the call came and she got the piece for nearly $300 less than the original asking price—the owner needed space for new merchandise and was ready to move out the big buffet. The result of this bargain? She is as loyal to the shop as Elinor is to Marianne or as Eliza-beth is to Jane or as Dr. Grant is to his dinner. She keeps going back and tells others to shop there as well.

Now that you have created your dining area, how are you going to make that dinner or lunch? Generally, buy your kitchen and other household appliances on sale but new, to ensure that they are not on the brink of breaking down and causing stressful problems, because you do not know their history. One exception to this rule would be cases in which you're familiar with the source or care of the product or trust the seller. For example, if your friend, who is more obsessively careful in her habits than Fanny Price, is moving and has a refrigerator or washer and dryer in good condition for sale—snap them up!

If shopping for appliances and electronics at an outlet mall, be sure to check the warranties. If you have to return to the mall for service on an electronic item, the savings may disappear in the cost of travel. If the appliance you buy has issues, it may be less possible to apply pressure to a store an hour away than one

Be Ready for Big Buys

Major purchases such as furniture, appliances, and some home accessories are a big investment, even when bought at a discount, so it's especially important to plan ahead and do research. Mary Bennet would be happy to assist you in this endeavor. Consult consumer reports on product reliability at the library or online, or look at webzines or blogs. Search in the newspapers and magazines for the best buys based on advertised sales. Check manufacturers' recalls as well. There's no sense buying an item only to return it. Then go out and enjoy shopping, knowing that the money you spend will be almost as well spent as if you bought another set of Austen's novels.

in your hometown, which will likely be more responsive to your problems.

Another option for new appliances is to check out a store that sells new but slightly damaged appliances, with warranties. Who cares if it's scratched or dented if you get a huge discount on a good-quality stove? Note where the damage is located on the appliance in relation to where it will be positioned in your home—it may be completely hidden or on the most obscured side in relation to most of the room, and you can always touch it up with a bit of paint. Think of Elinor smoothing over Marianne's rudeness or Lady Middleton discouraging her mother's vulgarity. When decorating your dining area or eat-in kitchen, remember that lighting can dramatically enhance the ambiance and your companions' enjoyment of the delectable food and hospitality you extend. Essential to the elegance of the space is the perfect chandelier. Tasteful chandeliers are more likely to appear at nicer thrift boutiques and antique consignments or through an individual seller's listing than at your neighborhood thrift store (though you never know—we know someone who got a charming green glass one for $5; we were filled with thrift envy). You may be able to strike a bargain with an antique consignment shop for a chandelier that's been hanging in the shop for several months or more, or for two light fixtures from the same consigner at an even bigger price cut. At least for a dining room, try to get one with real crystals (you'll see rainbow colors shining in them when lit). Even Caroline Bingley and Mrs. Hurst won't look askance at your hypnotizing crystalline wonder, sparkling with innumerable dainty beads and teardrops (though they'll privately joke about how you bought it with income you earned in trade).

What else will make your dining area radiant? Two words: silver plate. Sterling is not essential to elegance, no matter what Fanny Dashwood may say. An assortment of vintage silver-plated trays, teapots, cream and sugar sets, and bowls and pitchers in diverse styles and graduated sizes makes a stunning display in even the plainest possible hutch. Trust us—your entire collection can come from thrift stores, rummage sales, and garage sales (and the occasional gift, as friends discover your fetish). Then you can spend the rest of your life polishing it (or preferably, having your servants polish it). A prosperous friend of ours polishes her silver herself, as penance (and it works, good woman!).

Elaborate candlesticks or candelabra make wonderful accessories for the table or sideboard and can be found at all kinds of thrift stores and sales. The more ornate, the better—just keep an eye on Fanny Dashwood and Mrs. Ferrars. They may take it unkindly that you have something so nice and suggest that it really belongs at Norland or was theirs to begin with. Don't believe her if Fanny suggests she'll "step into the next room"

Don't be in the Dark

When considering used lighting, be aware that the lovely lamp that is exactly suited to your room of choice may need rewiring—if you get it for a song, it may be worth it. Get a precise estimate of the cost of any necessary repair or rewiring, however. Lighting experts often charge by the socket, so factor this in when considering buying a vintage chandelier with eight light sockets.

with the prettiest pair "to give dear John more light to read his paper" . . . you'll soon be hearing horses' hooves as she absconds with your treasures.

Tablecloths, drapes, and curtains can all be purchased used, are often available in good shape at charity boutiques, and can often be used interchangeably. A long curtain or even a patterned sheet or quilt can become a tablecloth if the fabric is opulent-looking enough (or you can place a translucent lace tablecloth over the top, thus disguising and dressing it up). Conversely, a striking iridescent, two-toned, jewel-colored tablecloth can become dining room curtains.

THE LIBRARY SPACE

Like Elinor and her family, you love to be surrounded by books, including a complete set of Jane Austen's novels, naturally. You must create a cozy but distinguished library space somewhere in your home that everyone can enjoy (not just Mr. Bennet!). Every respectable estate has one for the edification of its residents and as a legacy to future generations; a library would be an important resource for a parson in preparing sermons as well. Though ousted from their family estates, Elinor and Edward are both deep thinkers who cherish reading and quiet contemplation. If you don't have the space to devote an entire room to your passion for reading, it's easy to endow your ordinary family room, den, or even bedroom (or a designated corner of any room) with an urbane library feel on the cheap. Buy bookcases that fit the scale of the room or corner you've chosen, preferably real wood bookcases from an estate sale, auction, or consignment shop. Or, buy any bookshelves you can find and paint them a rich mahogany color. If they lack decorative features and you want to make your space more ornate, you can paint neoclassical columns down the sides or leafy Rococo flourishes to crown the top.

In addition to bookcases, your special reading space needs at least one chair that you can't resist sinking into with a copy of *Sense and Sensibility*. Inviting recliners or high-back chairs can be bought at cheap thrifts for cheap but may need to be spot-cleaned (no guarantees) or covered, and unless you can sew them yourself, slipcovers are often absurdly overpriced and cancel out the bargain of cheap furniture. Spend a little more and you'll usually get nicer-looking chairs, but beware of used furniture that is lovely but uncomfortable, like Lucy Steele—pretty on the outside but hard as steel on the inside. The best bet is to get comfortable, attractive furniture in good condition with minor, "clean" damage—Kathleen found an ultra-comfy recliner in like-new shape with one mark on the less noticeable side (not on the seat), for $40! Colonel Brandon or Anne Elliot would be perfectly willing to sit in it and politely suggest mind-expanding reading to further our maturation.

To accessorize your library area, of course you're going to fill the bookshelves, especially with handsome older editions of classics, favorites from your childhood, and etiquette and conduct books to keep you decorous. Okay—and a few carefully chosen new books as well (including, for example, this one). Scan all thrift venues for your favorite novels and essay and poetry collections, some with charming illustrations (just say no to Reader's Digest Condensed Books, however: you have your pride). On occasion, a personal library of merit is for sale in its entirety through an auction or estate sale. Individual volumes of etiquette and other specialty books can sometimes be found at consignment gift shops as well.

Ideally, the room that houses your library should have a wood or convincing laminate floor and a rich color on the walls that also predominates in the plush area rug, enhancing the Old World atmosphere of cultured comfort. Perch a reproduction green library lamp (available new and reasonably priced at office supply stores) and a French phone on your desk. Antique phones can be pricey, but tasteful imitations are occasionally available at boutique thrift stores or sold new and distinctively decorated at nicer discount stores the likes of Stein Mart. Perhaps a quill-and-ink set or a bust of Jane Austen belongs on the bookcases. Pick up zany bookends at most thrifts for a song, whether back-and-front mallards, bespectacled moose in evening suits, or even idiosyncratic zebra ones that Mr. Palmer selects with decision and hands over to you without a word or an expression on his face. Flea markets and garage sales can be especially productive of such unique home accents.

BEDROOMS AND BATHROOMS

The same principles of furnishing and decorating that you exercise in the social areas of your house or apartment apply to any sleeping area and bathroom in your home, whether for your own or your guests' use. They should be comfortable places with a restful, refreshing, but personalized atmosphere reminiscent of a luxury hotel (but without its anonymity and lofty price tag).

You should always buy mattresses new, but you may be able to claim a plush, high-end bed at a big discount because it's the floor model and the movers caused minor damage to it. Make sure it is, in fact, a new bed and that the damage is something you can fix or live with (scam sales do happen in which used goods are packaged as new or flaws are concealed, like Willoughby masking his sordid past, but floor models are unwrapped and easy to scrutinize while on display). Then get a striking secondhand bed frame or headboard at an estate sale, auction, or charity thrift boutique. You may find a wonderful sleigh bed or poster bed, or a headboard with a fantastical carved design. Don't be afraid to mix woods, as long as the bed frame, dresser, vanity, and any shelves are similar tones. Wood varnishes, scuff removers, or oil can work wonders as well. Bedside tables, like living room side tables, are a bit difficult to find used in matching pairs, and the ones at basic thrifts are usually spares, so be on the watch for these and don't expect to find a set you like instantaneously. Perhaps this thrift challenge is a metaphor for the struggle to find the right match in life—poor Elinor had to wait a long time to pair off with Edmund, who didn't "match" Lucy at all!

Most bathrooms require little in the way of furniture, and it can be cheap—you're not going to host a ball in there. Pick up cute little cabinets, supply shelves, or a stool on clearance at a discount department or home improvement store, or buy them used made of wood, wicker, or iron, and paint them to match your décor. For linens, purchase crisp new towels and sheets that will wear well. Discount stores are wonderful places to search for bedding, towels, drapes, housewares, and trendy pampering products. They often send out coupons that make the deep discounts ever deeper—Bed Bath & Beyond stores routinely mail out 20 percent off coupons that can make shopping at their stores a real bargain. They carry brand-name merchandise at a discount, and their overall discount coupon makes that vacuum cleaner or bedding set an even better value. Many thrifty shoppers carry the coupon around with them "just in case." If the occasion arises, they're all set.

For cost-effective planning for your shopping excursion, some discount stores like HomeGoods offer soft goods such as bedding and curtains as well as small furniture and accessories. They are often linked with discount stores that feature clothing for the whole family as well, so the shopper can find a wider variety of items in a single location. That represents a savings in time, transportation costs, and discounted merchandise— imagine having to pay for the coachman to bring out the horses and drive to different shops every time you want to look for pillowcases, placemats, and shoes. Outlet stores may also be a good bet for a striking comforter set. Get the highest thread count of cotton sheets you can for the best price (bedding comes with the mattress purchase at some bed stores, but check its quality before assuming this is a perk—no yucky polyester blends). After all her self-denial, Elinor deserves a good night's sleep in as much comfort as her modest means allow!

Luxurious accents can make both you and your guests feel pampered. Find a pretty piece of fabric and fold it at the foot of each bed, like at a hip hotel (but yes—it's really a tablecloth or drape from an estate sale). Elinor and Edward would have provided expensive but desirable scented soap from the Pears

Company for their guests. Pay the price and put good soap in each bathroom. You may consider up to four dollars per soap well spent on natural bars whose rose or carnation essence you can inhale daily and be transported to the gardens at Norland. The soap should be a color that accentuates the décor and a pleasant natural fragrance that's strong enough to freshen the room. Consider making your own—Susan made adorable lavender-scented glycerin soaps with molds for Christmas gifts, in the shape of winged cherubs. A small but punchy scented candle can serve as potpourri as well. Mix and match towel and washcloth colors as long as they coordinate with the bathroom décor (this enables you to work with what you have over the years; well-made towels last a while and, if carefully laundered, keep their color fairly well).

A great way to get fresh interior design ideas is to visit displays at more expensive stores or stores whose style appeals to your tastes, and then either buy your favorite elements of their display on sale, or re-create their look from similar pieces you pick up elsewhere at a fraction of the cost. Hip stores like Anthropologie often have charming displays of home décor items from which you may draw inspiration, as well as sale corners that may appeal to you.

With home decorating, as with everything else, there comes a time when all the elements of your creative exertion converge to produce the longed-for results (if only this happened for us as consistently as it did for our beloved genius, Jane!). For example, you've had it with the endless futile search for a rug that suits your strangely long, narrow bathroom. Everything is the wrong dimensions and remarkably ugly (who designs these rugs? Do they awaken from their nightmares and promptly sketch the mockups?). Then, from a distance, you see it. Your spirit soars to new heights as you rush forward, seize the rug—with its subtle but pleasing three-toned pattern and plush texture—and at long last have a vision of your finished bathroom. You take it to the towel department and splurge on one large towel and two small ones in your favorite shade on the rug pattern, and buy all four items with the 20 percent off coupons you've been saving up. As soon as you walk in your door, you gather a few added accessories in colors that also coordinate well with the rug (such as a carnival glass candy dish for potpourri and a funky framed photo), and then put all of the puzzle pieces in place as if in a trance. You step back to discover that with your help, the bathroom has found itself. It feels chastened from its former aesthetic rebellion and aspires to be more like you, who are the Elinor to its Marianne: serene in dignified beauty and the calm knowledge of right. In short, you love your reformed bathroom. Friends who come over on a Friday night after work declare with envy that you have a spa like the interior design shows. They linger fondly over the pleasing tones and textures, unable to comprehend exactly why they can't seem to leave the bathroom behind, even knowing they are missing the exchange of countless clever Austen allusions in the drawing room.

Entertaining and Hosting

Now that your home is beautifully furnished and decorated on way less than anyone would ever guess and welcomes in guests with its refined comfort, it's time to consider what to offer them.

HOSTING MEALS

Entertaining is a teachable craft. In the realm of dining, as in the realm of décor, some expenses are worthwhile and others are not. For example, when making hors d'oeuvres, consider that generic crackers taste like damp paper, but gourmet water crackers are crisp, flaky discs of salty goodness, topped with a slice of brie and a dollop of mildly sweet fig jam made from your own figs (how are Elinor's feelings to be described on consuming such a treat?). Common humanity for one's guests and oneself makes the choice crystal-clear.

Price does not always determine yumminess, however. For breakfast, today's Elinor would make her overnight guests cheap but crowd-pleasing, from-scratch pancakes or waffles made with a good old-fashioned waffle iron. You can throw in nutmeg, banana chunks, or walnuts (gathered with devotion by Harriet Smith's Mr. Martin, no doubt) or set out a variety of fruit and nut toppings. Guests will enjoy participating in creating their breakfast, and it will help them wake up. For lunch, simple sandwiches are fine as long as they begin with fresh bread, like baguettes from an authentic French bakery. For a healthy snack between meals, set out a basket of apples from Donwell Abbey. For a casual supper, shake things up and please especially visitors with kids by making a homemade "TV dinner." There are many options, but we suggest well-seasoned turkey burgers, homemade mac 'n' cheese, and strained peas. Serve in varied colors of vintage plastic plates with sections, and inspire nostalgic smiles. "TV dinners" are showing up on the menu at hip restaurants and really hit the spot on a chilly day.

As for the formal evening dinner party, chicken is a perfectly respectable as well as economical choice of entrée and can be prepared in a myriad of ways and accompanied by a potato or rice dish, a vegetable, and a pretty garnish. Simple, flavorful meals satisfy a variety of palates. Lasagna is another good choice and works well as a vegetarian dish (you could serve a classic, tomato-based meat version and a spinach version with red or white sauce). Gone are the days when guests expect an expensive cut of meat for the entrée. And do we care what Mr. Palmer "expects"? He'll eat what we serve or be banished to the time-out corner with an outdated newspaper, no droll remarks allowed! Brainstorm ideas by flipping through the many intriguing cookbooks for sale at thrift stores, and while you're at it, buy some for Aunt Norris (for her new life of seclusion with the disgraced Maria, after their mutual ill will drives away every cook to be found).

When to ignore "vulgar economy" when it comes to food and drink?

❧ Get the good coffee and make it at home, or go to your favorite coffee shop and bring home special orders. For tea drinkers, get loose-leaf tea and make it the traditional way. If you're planning to serve wine, ask the wine seller to suggest a moderately priced selection that matches your meal. You can also obtain recommendations in the wine department at your grocery store.

❧ Always serve only fresh-baked breads and rolls, whether made by you or someone else.

❧ Serve good, real butter (whether Irish, Danish, or domestic). There is nothing like real butter. Remember that it's often the smaller splurges that make the meal.

❧ The dessert must be exquisite. There is a few dollars' difference between frozen artificially flavored ice with food coloring and toxic chemicals and real sorbet made with fruit juice. Similarly, pick real ice cream over mystery freeze.

❧ Most important, absolutely no prepackaged bulk cookies. People eat them only as an act of desperation, when there is nothing else and all hope is gone. If you can't bake from scratch, your only options are to cut and bake cookies on the fly from frozen dough or buy from the bakery.

❧ When hosting guests for a meal, always ask about allergies. You may want to casually run down a dinner menu ("I was thinking of serving smelts, pickled pigs' feet, rutabaga mash, and dandelion greens with anchovy chutney. What do you think?"). If you're Mrs. Jennings, you'll do your best to extort a confession of their preferring salmon to cod, or boiled fowls to veal cutlets.

Setting the Table

Presentation goes a long way to creating an overall feeling of opulence. People aren't used to formal dinners any more. China is often omitted from today's bridal registries in favor of casual dinnerware. Fortunately for those with finer taste, there is

much china in the thrift world. You have no excuse not to possess lovely china. The challenge is to find a set you like that has
few or no missing pieces and little to no damage. But choose a
pattern you like over the quest for perfection, and feel free to
mix and match partial sets or individual settings. We know an
Austen lover who has all different plates and tea cups in a variety of shabby-chic-style rose patterns. Many thrift stores have
partial sets—if you combine two china sets to have a sufficient
number for larger parties, pick sets in designs and colors that
work well together (alternate the place settings—one plate has a
center bouquet and a gold rim, while the other has only a border
design but in similar shades of green, pink and gold).

Church rummage sales are a good place to look for beautiful
china and glassware, which people often donate when they're
moving to a smaller place. The donors feel generous, they clean
out their cupboards, and they may get a deduction on their
income taxes. Thanks to their generosity, we've bought everything from Wedgwood to Waterford at deeply discounted
prices, and you, too, can buy fine tableware with no buyer's
remorse because you bought it for pennies on the dollar. Outlet
malls also offer dishes and glassware by famous makers; even
Mrs. Ferrars might have deigned to purchase a flashing Waterford Irish cut crystal epergne vase there, if she got a good price.
For casual everyday dishes, discount stores often carry festive
sets with appealing fruit, floral, or abstract patterns.

To complement your china, you will need attractive flatware
that reflects your taste. You can choose sterling, silver plate, or
stainless steel; lovely patterns of well-made and balanced eating
utensils are available in each of these materials. Each material
has its advantages and disadvantages. Sterling is beautiful and

develops a patina over time; the downside is that sterling is expensive and requires polishing to be at its most beautiful. Less expensive silver plate (utensils made with a silver layer over a less expensive metal) offers a wide variety of patterns with the wonderful luster of silver, but it also requires polishing. Stainless steel is generally least expensive and easiest to maintain, and many of the sterling and silver plate manufacturers produce appealing stainless patterns as well.

Desirable sets of silver plate can sometimes be found at estate sales for around $50, and occasionally for less at nicer thrift shops; they also appear at auctions and antique stores. When shopping for flatware of any kind, be sure to lift the individual pieces and see how they feel in your hand; many beautiful patterns may not be very well balanced when you use them, thus detracting from the eating experience, especially if you are entertaining. As with china, you can also mix and match silverware. We would not recommend mixing different flatware patterns at one place setting, but you can alternate matching sets at every other place. Make sure utensils are in good condition, both attractive and without corroded or worn-through patches that won't polish away (or that would cut even Lucy Steele's smug mouth). A miscellany of serving spoons as well as platters for parties can easily be found at the cheap thrift shop.

Dressing Up as Hostess

How does a lady look her best, especially on a limited income caused by the injustice of the law of primogeniture? How can she conceal her skimpy budget and dress to honor the occasion?

When dressing for dinner, it's perfectly fine to sport a solid-color thrift store dress in good-quality fabric, with an artificial pearl necklace and earrings (available everywhere cheap). The only expensive part of your ensemble is the low-heeled dress shoes with good cushioning and comfortable fit. You are ready to parley with your parishioners or even to regale royalty. No one will know that the entire outfit (minus the shoes) cost less than Mrs. Ferrars's left stocking. Your look of classic sophistication commands respectful admiration and subdues even Willoughby, that self-indulgent dog!

Cultured Entertainment

A genteel, cultured lady encourages her friends to participate in a variety of mind-expanding pleasures. Music is one of her favorite modes of entertainment. Encourage your guests to bring their instruments or pass around some of your own and gather around for an impromptu concert. Those with musical gifts, like Marianne, are often willing to share them. A harmonious blend of such sounds as piano, guitar, ukulele, recorder, harmonica, drums, and the human voice will inspire everyone, whether they're playing, singing, or listening.

You can also play a variety of brain-sharpening games with family and friends, such as charades, word puzzles, and other games of wit. Elinor, like Anne Elliot in *Persuasion*, isn't much of a card player; however, she joins tables as needed to complete the group and enable others to play. One could always learn whist or Chance, and Mr. Palmer would no doubt provide encouragement in the form of blunt criticism.

And if the guys occasionally need to slip away to Edward's "man cave" in the stable, where Colonel Brandon and Sir John trounce their host and an ever-so-briefly humbled Mr. Palmer at a few rounds of darts, we don't mind. They have a small fridge and snack supply at the ready, knowing full well that no self-respecting Elinor of the present age will be sashaying in with trays of beer and nachos.

As all hosts know, engaging in witty banter can also provide inspiration. Reading aloud can be a pleasant pastime for the family circle, and we're sure Edward can improve his style with application and coaching from Marianne. And yes, Fanny Price, one can participate in private theatricals, but only if the play is a very proper one, we promise!

Clearly, a refined and even modestly luxurious lifestyle can be created on a budget. One doesn't need to be extravagant and expect high-end everything. Just know which investments are worthwhile and which aren't, and how to create overall effects and experiences for your loved ones and yourself without being a big spender. Subtle details make a difference. Like Jane Austen and her wise heroine, Elinor, you live a sensible, frugal lifestyle and economize in most areas most of the time. But when it's time to celebrate, to express your joie de vivre, you "eat ice and drink French wine," and save "vulgar economy" for tomorrow.

How elated our long-enduring Elinor must have been to have the opportunity to make her companions a return for their generous hospitality during her family's time of struggle and grief. Finally settled at the parsonage with her beloved Edward, secure in his love and Marianne's restored health, she turns her energies to making a home and gathering her circle of friends in it. We follow her example of economical elegance in our own place and time. We become practical princesses, domestic fairies who throw open the doors of our humble dwellings and welcome in the Mrs. Jenningses, Charlotte Palmers, Colonel Brandons, and Sir John Middletons of our own lives. Steeles and Willoughbys need not apply!

Chapter 9

Austen-tatious Antique Sales, Auctions, Estate Sales, and Flea Markets

*"The rooms were lofty and handsome,
and their furniture suitable to the fortune of
their proprietor"*

If you are especially eager to re-create Jane Austen's world or the world of the novels in your own home, the best place to start looking for the furnishings, the silver and crystal, the dishes, the clothing, and the books that populate the fictional Regency is at an antique sale, auction, estate sale, or flea market. To maximize the likelihood of scoring great deals on unique pieces for home and family, you must understand the inner workings of each venue.

Antique Shows

At least one weekend a month in almost any locale, you can find an antique show within driving distance of your home. The beauty of an antique show is the variety of dealers it attracts, ranging from those with small items such as jewelry and dishes to those selling huge sideboards and armoires. Because the dealers often come from all over the country, they often sell a wider variety of antiques than local shops or sales might offer. Even better, antique shows display the very finest examples of the artistry and craftsmanship of the past, because the dealers offer items that provide the highest profit to offset overhead and travel expenses.

Imagine the opportunity to re-create Elizabeth Bennet Darcy's drawing room at Pemberley, or to furnish the breakfast room at Longbourn with the beautiful furniture, linens, and table settings you imagine from Austen's novels or from the films they inspire. The antique show will offer glimpses of Austen's world, from the charming table furnishings and china sets that Austen and her characters lingered over at tea to the tastefully designed and proportioned furniture Fitzwilliam Darcy selected or conserved for his elegant family home.

Of course, unless you're Lady Catherine de Bourgh or Fanny Dashwood, the antique show can be an intimidating experience. There are so many booths to visit, and the dealers are usually so knowledgeable in their specialty areas that it's hard for a beginning collector or buyer to approach them. However, most dealers, especially those who have spent much time and care on the pieces they have to offer, are more than willing to share their expertise with potential customers, particularly if you have a special project in mind, such as furnishing a specific room or acquiring a tea set in a pattern you cherish or glassware from a period like the Regency. For the dealer, working with a beginner means the opportunity to develop a profitable future relationship.

As with all sales adventures, be sure to decide ahead of time what you're looking for. If you are planning to buy anything at the antique show, doing research in advance will repay your effort. You will recognize the kinds of things you like and learn the vocabulary of collecting them. Consulting any one of the specialized price guides for antiques will give you an idea of current values so you can make an informed decision about prices. If you want a set of chairs, learn the terminology of their construction. Be able to discuss your potential purchase intelligently. Many times dealers have other items for sale that they didn't bring to the show; these might be your dream purchase. Henry Tilney is always looking for quality muslin and picturesque paintings, so he will inquire if the dealers have any. If dealers are not local, you can often contact them through the Internet, and many will be on the lookout for your desired items, eager to make a sale and to assist you in your collecting.

Decide on a plan when you enter the show hall. Don't miss any of the displays. It's good to go to the antique show with a friend because each of you can call the other's attention to items

An Antiquarian Education

Many antique shows have lectures and presentations on such topics as antiques for home design, spotting fakes, insuring your collectible items, and refinishing. The price of admission to the show itself will give you special insight into many facets of the antique world you had not even considered, making the admission well worth your investment.

of interest, and if you have a hard time deciding whether you should buy something, a friend can provide advice or encouragement. It's better when you have a friend who has collecting interests different from yours. When Elinor and Marianne go to the antique show, Marianne will be looking for Romantic poetry and piano music, while Elinor will be carefully examining decorative fire screens.

Some of the best buys can be found in the antique show because dealers know and label what they have, and they ordinarily stand behind the quality and authenticity of their wares. Always ask whether the marked price is the best available; many dealers will lower the cost if asked, usually around a 10 percent discount. However, don't try to make a very low offer for an item you want, even if you think the price is out of line. Offending a dealer is a sure guarantee that you won't be receiving any bargains in the future at that booth. Lucy, don't try to steal that thread case you covet by naming an absurd amount; you'll only lose in the end. And the dealers talk, so you can get a reputation that's hard to live down.

You can also sell antique items that you don't want any more at an antique show. Many dealers expect to buy and sell at the shows. Have an informed price in mind when you offer your item for sale; many dealers will not make an offer unless they have an idea of what you want for what you're selling. Don't be offended if the dealer isn't interested. Dealers know what they can sell because they are constantly in the marketplace; when they buy from you, they have to factor in their time, overhead, and profit margin for a reasonable selling price. Don't expect a retail price when selling to someone who has to resell an item.

Antique Shops

If you are collecting and decorating with antiques, you probably want to visit antique shops as well. Dealers can often tell you where an item comes from (its provenance). Many dealers specialize in antiques they know will appeal to their regular customers, so you may find that if you want to match a china pattern, one dealer will have just the piece you want. Another dealer will offer furniture; another, antique jewelry. Each of these dealers will have done the study necessary to evaluate the pieces being sold and to inform the customer regarding any questions.

Develop a relationship with a local dealer. Ask questions about the things in the shop and buy something when you visit. Dealers are often more generous in dealing with regular customers who provide repeat business, and they also have lots of interesting tales to tell about the treasures they offer for sale. Also, dealers may be able to let you know about items of interest elsewhere, especially in shops with specialties different from theirs. Shops often support each other's business, in your interest and theirs.

Antique Malls

What could be better than an antique shop for bargain hunting? An antique mall. Finding your way into Austen's world through a series of cases supplied by different dealers can make you one moment a Lucy Steele, admiring the variety of Regency needle books available at an advantageous price, the next moment a

Robert Ferrars, selecting just the right toothpick case from a drawer full of these eccentric items.

Antique malls bring together the goods offered by a variety of dealers in one shopping experience. Malls ordinarily rent cases to a number of sellers, who are responsible for pricing their goods and maintaining the appearance of their displays. If the mall is a cooperative venture, dealers take turns handling the paperwork for all the purchases; if the mall is owned by one individual, that person provides one or more employees to process sales, ensure security, and find answers to questions.

If you are interested in selling some of your overflow at an antique mall, contracts usually require a rental fee for the booth and an additional percentage of the ultimate price of each sale. In return for this, the mall keeps track of all the sales made in the store and collects, documents, and remits state and local sales taxes (taking this bookkeeping burden off the sellers, many of whom are just selling things from their homes and families in a setting where they feel they can get the best price). Dealers at an antique mall may be professional dealers, who can maintain a sales space and do shows without the additional overhead required to run an antique store by themselves, or they may be amateurs who are downsizing their holdings in preparation to move or retire. The advantage in either case is that they have a place to display their wares in a permanent setting, so they don't have to be there to sell their items and secure them because there is a staff provided for that purpose, and they can be on the road, buying more stock, without worrying about what is happening back at the store. Because one of the most difficult parts of the antique business is maintaining a steady supply of inventory, many dealers like the antique mall for both its business efficiency and the camaraderie with other dealers. They can sneak in to rearrange the case, pick up their checks, or just share talk over coffee with the other dealers.

For buyers, one of the disadvantages of the mall is that the dealer may not be present when the buyer has questions to ask. If the dealer is not available, you may have to wait while an employee calls the dealer for information about an item's provenance or to negotiate a lower price. The Bingley sisters would simply walk off in a huff.

If you are looking for something special, such as a vintage edition of Austen or a hair ring like Lucy Steele gave Edward Ferrars, make sure to ask the sales staff which display case would be likely to yield the treasure you seek. Good antique malls have knowledgeable staff that know the merchandise and can direct you to a dealer who handles antique whirligigs, pinwheels, or diamond hairpins.

As always in shopping for treasures, be sure that you decide ahead of time on a buying strategy. If you are a Harriet Smith looking for a dining room table, don't be deflected by a vintage teddy bear that is priced the same as the furniture you want, no matter how cute it is. If you know you need to fill in a china pattern, be sure to look up online replacement values so you don't overpay, or so you recognize a bargain when you see one. Because dealers often buy goods in lots, they are not necessarily knowledgeable about every single thing they have for sale. Frequently, dealers' booths contain *sleepers*—items that the dealer didn't pay much for and didn't have time to research. Thus, it's possible to snatch a bargain even in the world of antiques and even if you aren't Lucy Steele. That's what makes for the excitement of the hunt at antique shows, shops, and malls.

Let the longing for the gracious manners and way of life of Austen's characters (except Lucy, of course) be your guide as you shop for antiques, but keep in mind that the thriftiest way to acquire the Regency lifestyle involves doing your homework, making connections with dealers, and deciding in advance what you are willing to spend. Sometimes it's better to pay more for something in pristine condition with a Pemberley provenance. Always, always ask for a discount, but always in the most genteel possible way: "I pray, sir, is this the best price?"

Tips:

- Get to know the antique dealers at the antique shows and the local shops or malls you visit. Dealers remember the people who buy from them (often by the item they purchased) and are glad to see a potential customer again. Because dealers are often experts in their areas of specialization, they are eager to boost your enthusiasm, too. The goodwill generated by sharing information makes the customer want to return.

- Dealers are willing to educate buyers, providing more than just the items they need, and that education can be the greatest bargain of all.

- Remember that everyone, even dealers, makes the occasional mistake in buying. There is nothing less to do than (like Lady Russell) admit to yourself that you have been pretty completely wrong. If you find you've overpaid, consider it tuition for the future.

❧ Keep trying to find your inner Austen. Keep learning, keep looking, and keep bargaining.

Auctions

We can embrace our inner Jane and do some clever interior decorating with buys found at the local auction house, as well as at flea markets and house sales where we can haggle for the things we want at the best possible price. For auctiongoers, a few rules will guarantee an enjoyable and profitable time. First, the buyer must understand that most auctions require buyers to register and have a number assigned to them. All purchases are recorded for that number, and at the end of the sale, the buyer settles her account for all items purchased. Be sure to know ahead of time the terms of the sale: cash only, cash or credit card only, or checks accepted with proper identification. Also note that most auction houses charge a buyer's premium, usually a percentage of the price, which is added to the winning bid (with sales tax, where appropriate, on top of all that). So, in calculating a bid, know that the actual price will be larger than what you are bidding, and the more expensive the item, the greater the price will be than the ending bid.

Look the items over ahead of time. Most auctions sell wares "as is," which means no returns. It's up to you to determine what you are looking at and what you want to pay for it. If you don't want to do repairs or if damage will significantly lower the value, don't bid. In fact, set a value in your head before the auction begins and don't bid above what you decide to pay. It's easy to get caught up in the competition of the auction—that's

Austen and Auctions

When Reverend James Austen, Jane's father, gave up his ministry to his son, the Austens had to downsize. Everything that would not be useful in Bath was to be sold, in a belt-tightening move to smaller quarters. The family would consign their goods to auction. Reverend Austen would sell his library. Jane would lose her beloved piano, which inspired her in her early writing; she then experienced a dry spell in her writing that lasted through her residence at Bath.

When Jane Austen's piano sold at auction, it fetched only £8 (a sum that she explained in a letter to her sister was all that she "really expected to get," although it represented only about 10 percent of the cost of a new Broadwood grand at the time). Her resignation in itself reflects a sense of disappointment for the loss of an instrument so important to her at so low a price. A set of tables brought an unsatisfactory "Eleven Guineas," although the family cows brought in considerably more.

Like many people consigning goods to auction, the Austens were disheartened by the results. Often, consigners feel the auctioneer was not energetic enough with the sale of their goods, or that the advertising of the sale was not sufficient to bring in the kind of crowd necessary for the maximum price.

At least the Austens weren't *forced* to sell their goods at auction but chose to sell them that way, because it was a popular way of reducing housekeeping. By contrast, in Austen's day, many families in reduced circumstances had their household possessions seized by the bailiffs and sold.

what the auctioneer's patter is all about. It's a good idea to stand on the sidelines so that if you are bidding, you can see where the auctioneer is taking the other bids. There are always rumors about syndicates of bidders that run the price up on an item, especially if the bidder is inexperienced and uninformed. Watch what you are doing—bidders indicate their offer by raising their number, calling out, and a wide variety of somewhat arcane hand gestures. If you're a Harriet Smith, beware of fluttering your hands in indecision over a purchase—you could accidentally become the proud owner of an antique chamber pot with original "patina" and empty every cent out of your savings. Set your ceiling price ahead of time and make a note on the items on which you wish to bid; that way you won't buy something on impulse or overpay, only to regret your purchase later.

Auctions range from high end to house auctions. Specialty auctions sell one sort of item such as dolls or paintings, so if those interest you, you can learn a lot from a specialty auction. Auction galleries have mixed sales and specialty sales. Local auctions sometimes include box lots, a kind of grab bag of interesting items mixed together indiscriminately. Harriet bids on a box lot and gets it for a few pence—imagine her surprise to find it includes a totally incomprehensible Charade, a piece of court plaster, and a book on orchard pruning with Mr. Martin's bookplate. She is elated. What a value.

Following the auction advertising in the newspapers will give you a good idea of whether an auction will feature your favorite categories of finds. Often, estate auctions will offer items belonging to a prominent or even famous person. Marianne will certainly want to attend the auction of Lord Byron's effects. Beware, however, such phrases in the advertising as "plus additions." They mean that many of the wares to be sold may be from other sources and have considerably less value, certainly in terms of celebrity but frequently in terms of age and quality. They are fill-ins that the auctioneer is including to amplify his profit.

Auctions offer excitement and fun. If Austen's characters were to go to the auction, how would we recognize them? Mrs. Norris will attempt to get the best goods for the cheapest prices. Watch her trying to make friends with the bookkeeper or the auction runners, in hopes of "spunging" an item or two for free. Or Lucy Steele will be there snaking through the crowd trying to distract and discourage other bidders: "La, these items are too dirty for me," she'll say, after she has smeared mustard from her hot dog all over a Sèvres vase. Then she'll steal it for next to nothing. Isabella Thorpe will be flirting with the runners and the auctioneer, batting her eyes and making sure she is in the way every time a piece of furniture is brought up for bid. "Did you see them looking at me?" she demands. "They really put me quite out of countenance." Willoughby will be intent on having his way, no matter what the cost.

Estate Sales

If the competition of auction fever is too intense for you and Harriet Smith, another way to find real bargains is to haunt estate sales. Although theoretically, these should offer bargains from one or more estates, the canny buyer must be aware that other, less authentic estate items may be added. In some places, estate sales are referred to as *tag sales*, although in general, tag sales may involve the sale of any merchandise, not just what is being dispersed from an estate.

True estate sales offer the excitement of finding items offered for sale that someone once treasured, possessions from a private home that have not been seen by many people. These may display an idiosyncratic collecting appetite—Lady Middleton's collection of esoteric sheet music or Sir John Middleton's statues of hunting dogs, perhaps—or they may just reveal the tastes of a Mrs. Bates or old Mrs. Smith in *Sense and Sensibility*. Sometimes estate sales offer a time capsule, revealing the details of a person's life and accomplishments. Estate sales may unearth items filled with nostalgia, such as unidentified family photographs and handwritten recipe books; they can equally well produce the trendy vintage collectibles of the future: sets of dishes or kitchen utensils given to newlyweds in the 1950s, for example, or desirable midcentury modern goods. A complete luncheon set of early 1950s Stangl Wild Rose pottery will delight the modern Charlotte Lucas Collins and enliven the table of the ranch-style parsonage; they remind her of lunches at Grandma's.

Aunt Norris eagerly scans the Thursday evening and Friday morning papers for the estate sales, which are frequently advertised along with the garage sales. They are mostly held on weekends, sometimes over Friday, Saturday, and Sunday. Often they take place in the home of the deceased, although some estate sales consist of goods that have been removed to a warehouse or other venue where they can be showcased more advantageously than in a house. Many times, estate sales will be run by professionals who tag and price all the items before the purchasers show up. If you love this kind of sale, it is definitely worthwhile to get on the mailing or calling (or e-mailing) list of these professionals so that you will receive word when a sale will be held with things of interest to you; important items such as John Thorpe's snuffbox or Willoughby's officer's uniform will often be described in detail and photographed for your review.

What are the best items to find at estate sales? Often estate sales held in houses will offer the opportunity to pick up sets of dinnerware, cookware, or glassware at a reasonable price. These are also good places to find tools for home maintenance and gardening. Distinctive urns for plants, statues of grinning garden gnomes, and lawn furniture may tempt you to decorate your garden at bargain prices. The sellers are eager to get rid of the contents of the house, and after the first day, both amateur sellers and professionals will often either take offers on higher-priced wares or bargain for any item at a reduced price (unless the price is *firm* or non-negotiable). Estate sales also feature furniture bargains because most professionals and other sellers want to get someone else to move bigger pieces off the property. Because one can frequently buy furniture with much better frames than what is offered in furniture stores today, sometimes it is worthwhile to purchase a piece of vintage furniture just to have it reupholstered to your taste. You get just the fabric, color, and style you want and still end up with a higher-quality item for a lower price than buying new.

Good estate sale professionals work their lists of buyers, so if the sale is expected to be spectacular, arrive there well before the starting time. Frequently lines of buyers will wait for half an hour or more for the privilege of getting into the sale first. Gather up the items that interest you and don't ever put them down. Anything that is not in the hands of a prospective buyer is likely to be scooped up and purchased by someone else, ever eager to find a steal. Often the first people in line are dealers, so don't be intimidated when in the salesroom or the house. Be sure to go to the things you like, and if you think the price is acceptable, make up your mind on your purchases quickly (or at least carry them around until you decide).

If you want a piece of furniture, let the sellers know right away. They will expect you to pay for it up front if they are to hold it for you. Experienced sellers don't want to be left with something someone has promised to return for and then changed her mind. For the most part, you will be expected to provide transportation for what you buy, although some sales professionals provide delivery service for a fee or direct you to truckers who will deliver your purchases for a reasonable charge.

Estate sales can be crowded, so they are not really for the claustrophobic (unless you come later in the day). Also, unless the sales organizers have had plenty of time to prepare the items, they may not be particularly clean. Come prepared for the weather—hot or cold—and come in clothing that you don't mind washing. We find that for bargaining purposes, it is sometimes better to look a little shabby rather than very fashionable. Don't be afraid to accentuate a limp or sigh dramatically periodically—we remember a dealer who used to claim she should be at the head of the waiting line because she had to use a cane (to keep other buyers from the good items, actually). Sellers size up the buyers and have lots of experience in buyer psychology, so if you want to get your prize at the lowest price, it's a good idea not to look either too eager or too well off.

Sometimes you will just luck into an estate sale by seeing a sign at the side of the road. Just be aware that "estate sale" can sometimes be a euphemism for "garage sale," but don't let that stop you from following every lead. Even the poorest selection of items may harbor a real gem.

Flea Markets

As for flea markets, they may range widely in terms of the merchandise sold and the people who are selling it. If you plan to attend a flea market, get a good idea ahead of time what you may find there. The Internet is a great resource to use in planning your day of thrifty shopping; that way you won't waste your time looking at low-quality items that won't interest you.

Flea markets offer a wide variety of vendors. They may sell new, cut-rate goods that are often either seconds or return items, or cheap goods bought at a closeout. Others offer produce from local growers but sold by retailers who can offer bargains because the flea market overhead is low. Still others have thrift items brought from a wide variety of venues including garage sales, storage unit auctions, and rummage sale remains.

Private sellers may also be at a flea market—some people want to hold their garage sale at a location other than their own home. A few of the reasons for this include subdivision rules regarding visitor parking and a strong desire for anonymity; an Anne Elliot or a Fanny Price wouldn't want people to know where she lives or what she has. Sellers set up booths or stalls that offer a variety of used and vintage items, sometimes even antiques, and they can reward the thrifty shopper well. In fact, the flea market in this case can save the buyer from driving around neighborhoods looking for sales. Imagine Edmund and Fanny Bertram thriftily furnishing the rectory at Thornton Lacey with flea market finds, saving many bales of hay per mile on transportation.

Some flea markets have special sections for antique dealers. These dealers usually sell the same kinds of offerings found at an antique show, but the bargaining room is better because the overhead at a flea market is frequently lower. As always, carefully examine every item that interests you, because purchases are generally sold as is and where they are. Flea market dealers will probably not take back items that you later discover have some sort of damage. Always ask about the condition of the item if you have any questions. At the best flea markets, we have found wonderful treasures: carved fossil mammoth ivory buttons in the shape of seals, bought by the original owner in the 1940s garment district in New York; a fabulous fish head pen holder made from Bennington pottery; and an antique pokerwork pyrography stool marked with the name *Fan*. Did it belong to Fanny Price?

Special Sales

Be on the lookout for special sales in your area. Where we live, there are frequent one-day sales at the fairgrounds where people can simply rent a space and sell their goods. These sales feature a wide variety of exciting finds—vintage and used clothing, furniture, rugs, dishes, tools, and almost anything that you want and need at bargain prices. This is the kind of sale you want to get to early in order to find the best bargains. At the end of the day, if there's anything left you want, your bargaining power gets even greater. It's the kind of sale that Lucy Steele would have loved the most.

Never be afraid to ask "Is this your best price?" or "Can you tell me something about this?" Sometimes you may know more about the item than the person who is selling it, but it's never a bad idea to find out all you can about what you want to buy. For example, if you are in the market for a rug, don't be afraid to ask such questions as whether it came from a home with pets or whether it was owned by a smoker. No one wants to bring home someone else's problem, whether it be odors or animal dander to which family members may be allergic.

In our area, there is also an annual market to which charities bring items to sell, often from their resale shops. Money for admission to the sale also funds these charities in the local community, so the buyer gets a double benefit from supporting local organizations and finding bargains. Sometimes these events collect canned food for local food pantries instead of charging an entry price, which also helps others while providing entry to a wonderful shopping extravaganza. The bottom line on antique sales, auctions, estate sales, and flea markets is that all of them can give a wonderful day's entertainment while offering rich opportunities to the thrifty shopper. The catch is that these are sales where *caveat emptor*, "let the buyer beware," should be the shopper's motto.

Some final tips for shopping at auctions, flea markets, or house, garage, and estate sales:

- ❧ Never buy something about which you are uncertain or something you don't really love. A great bargain is no bargain at all if you can't stand it when you get it home.

- ❧ Don't buy something you don't need.

- ❧ Don't buy a damaged item unless you have the skill to repair it, you know someone who will do the repairs reasonably, or you don't really care about the damage—you just want it. You don't save money by spending it; you save it by keeping it in your pocket.

Chapter 10

CATHERINE MORLAND'S LESSONS ON BEING A GRACIOUS GUEST AND SAVVY TRAVELER

"Will you come and see me?"

What if you seek an adventure farther from home than the fairgrounds or flea market warehouse and more varied amusements than shopping? What if you feel restless for change and long for new sights and experiences but are short on funds to feed your wanderlust? A resourceful heroine can go adventuring on a budget in a variety of ways. Why not do as Catherine Morland did and go on a visit to see family or friends?

Traveling to Estates

Catherine learned a lot from her stay at Northanger Abbey, the estate of her friends the Tilneys. Her dos and don'ts still apply to us on our own sojourns to see loved ones old and new. Staying at the homes of other people is an economical way to travel while enjoying good company. Change of scene and spending time with those we care about (or may even hope to marry some day) have their own rewards, even if it means a lengthy carriage ride, sleeping at a scary mansion, or adhering to strict mealtimes. One can certainly vacation creatively in the present age on little money for maximum memories. This is fortunate, especially if one has nine siblings, a father with a modest parish living, a small dowry, and a sense of sameness and boredom that are kept at bay only by the incessant consumption of more Gothic novels than is good for one.

If you are flying to see your relative or friend, be sure to compare flights and prices before settling on a ticket. And if you are driving and must rent a car, carefully consider rental car prices. See "On Your Own Dime" later in this chapter for information on how best to gauge prices and save on travel.

PACK WITH PRECISION

As you prepare for your journey, pack your trunk carefully (yes, there is a correct way, according to Lady Catherine de Bourgh). To avoid those steep airline fees for checked bags, limit yourself to a carry-on suitcase, plus a bag with room for your laptop, purse or wallet, and copy of *The Mysteries of Udolpho*. If driving, pack one large suitcase and a floppy bag in which you can easily arrange awkward-to-pack stuff such as shoes, a raincoat, art supplies for sketching scenic overlooks, and of course, as many novels as you can pile in. Whether flying, driving, or being spirited away at incredible speed by villains in a traveling-chaise and four, be sure to pack your own snacks as well. For example, rather than buying the airline's overpriced packaged trail mix or cheesy crackers that are loaded with saturated fats, sugars, and salts, the night before your trip, mix together dried berries, pumpkin seeds, and coconut flakes with your nut of choice and divide into a number of Ziploc bags. This will save you money and heartburn, so you can offer your bottle of antacids to General Tilney instead.

TOKEN OF THANKS

You can express your appreciation to your hosts with a thoughtful act or object. Take them out to dinner at their favorite restaurant. Or buy the groceries and make them a special dinner at home, if they're comfortable with a visitor in the kitchen (a Greek friend made us a fabulous Greek dinner). Jane and her sister Cassandra often provided free babysitting when visiting their brothers with children, or they hosted one or more children at their house. In the novels, Harriet Smith helps with the kids when she stays with Isabella and John Knightley, Anne Elliot cares for the Musgrove boys, and Jane Bennet probably spends a lot of time with her little Gardiner cousins while in London. We know what you're thinking—that's not a vacation. But you have to choose a gesture that suits your talents and personality (child care would not be our choice, either, especially if the kids are anything like Lady Middleton's). Get into the spirit of your hosts' lives and what they find important, meaningful, or fun. If they're zealous gardeners, be as willing as Fanny Price to cut the roses, or even to help weed and pick tomatoes. If Frank Churchill wants to sing duets, do your best (just remember that he's not interested, no matter how much he flirts with you).

If you prefer to bring a present, keep it simple and modest in price range. Your hosts are extending their hospitality to you and will want to make your visit a treat, so don't make them feel awkwardly overcompensated for their generosity with an extravagant gift. If you don't know them well, a fruit basket or bottle of wine (if you're unaware of an issue in this area) or flower arrangement is appropriate. If you're crafty, a personalized gift of organic soaps or a birdhouse will be a unique surprise. But don't give something too décor-specific—they may fail to appreciate the lampshade you painted all over with miniature images of John Thorpe's pudgy, impudent face.

A GRACIOUS GUEST

Of course, the main motive of your visit to the estates of friends and relatives is to spend time with loved ones. The added bonus of an inexpensive adventure trip is the icing on the scone. Be as pleasant and flexible as Catherine Morland, accompanying your hosts on their outings to the pump room, concert, and theater and gladly joining in their favorite walks. Entertain your hosts. Be sociable and witty (okay; wit is not Catherine's strong point—she knows nothing of the picturesque!). Show your pleasure in your hosts' company. If they offer to escort you on day trips, pay for their museum admission (being strictly mercenary, you would have had to pay for transportation and tickets for yourself, anyway, along with hotel and all meal expenses and tips).

Think of your hosts as resident experts on the place you're visiting—benefit from their knowledge and experience of the area. They know the most stunning sights, the yummiest mom-

and-pop dives, the most characteristic cultural distinctives of their town. If you're in the Midwest, let the Gardiners take you on a tour of the breathtaking Great Lakes, capped off with a fish fry in their quaint resort town. When you go to New York, accompany Lady Dalrymple and the Honorable Miss Carteret to an opera at the Met, where they have the best box seats in the house. If you take a cruise, especially to the East Indies, be sure to travel with the Crofts—they're always at home on board ship!

No matter how long you've known someone, going for a visit gives you a chance to get to know him or her better. Being invited into someone's living space reveals more interesting insights about one's loved ones than many a conversation can do. You may admire anything that is left out in full view. However, if a door is kept shut and you are clearly told that guests are not welcome to enter that mysterious upstairs room, please resist the temptation, no matter how fascinating a portrait may be hidden therein; you must also resist the urge to dig in drawers or open a trunk in search of ancient scrolls.

As Catherine learned the hard way, don't be quick to judge your host. Follow his mealtime hours and stay on his good side (plus if he's the parent of someone with whom you're infatuated, you want to keep him charmed). Compliment the size of every room in his house and the extent of his grounds, and show enthusiasm even for his modern office building, though it was built well after the fifteenth century. Especially on an extended stay, taking some outings on your own will also give your hosts a break (let's face it—our sweetness and congeniality are charming enough, but our stupidity gets old).

What if your beneficent former boss, to whom you owe so

much of your current success, now lives not far from the friends (let's say a girlfriend and her charming brother) you're visiting at their parents' place in the Hamptons? Is it okay to ditch your host family for your former employer? Only if your visit to your hosts lasts at least a weekend, you've asked their input ahead of time, and the rendezvous is short (such as coffee). Make it clear that you're here primarily to see your hosts (whose guest room you're occupying, whose mansion you're secretly exploring, whose multicourse meals you're consuming, and whose nearly handsome, righteous son you plan to marry). What's not okay is for you to agree to an excursion with them, but then go off gallivanting to Blaize Castle with someone else instead.

Lessons to Learn from Austen's Worst Guests:

- ❧ Marianne Dashwood: Do not tour someone's house uninvited, even if the homeowner's nephew is cute and encourages it. Do not avoid or ignore your hosts or make yourself a burden to them. Thus, you must refrain from trudging off alone through the rainy countryside and making yourself seriously ill because some worthless slime jilted you (you're well rid of him and should now make yourself available for a worthy suitor—wake up and look around you!). Refusing to eat and sulking in tearful silence are also unacceptable.

- ❧ Mr. Collins: Though you may be a respectable man, don't assume that all single female members of the household you're visiting would be thrilled to marry you. Remember that the purpose of a social visit, realistically, should not be to propose to someone you have never met before.

Also, avoid forcing your acquaintance on anyone, and pay attention to the rules of a card game so you don't mess up and ruin your friends' play. Work on your dance steps before trying to impress a potential mate. Oh yes— and don't be a pompous fool.

❧ Mr. Palmer: It's best not to bluntly critique the home of one's host and to call him "as stupid as the weather" if he doesn't own a billiards table. You'll live. Perhaps you could focus on endeavoring to be genuinely droll.

❧ The Steele sisters: Try not to be an insincere user who strings together as many free visits as possible from any relative, friend, or near-stranger that will let you in the door.

Lessons to Learn from Austen's Best Guests:

❧ Anne Elliot: Be a blessing to your hosts. What better way to do this than by saving a life? If an accident or illness occurs while you're visiting, be the quick thinker who acts decisively and ministers to the patient with calm skill. Be the supportive presence in the family, the healing salve, the sympathetic listener, the resident family therapist (okay, don't let this role go too far—they can vent a little basic stress, but if they start oversharing, promptly offer to play the piano for dancing). You're such a good person that your presence eases tensions and inspires accord. But don't be too selfless—suffering ages your complexion.

❧ Elinor Dashwood: When visiting others, one has an obligation to be polite and sociable. Respect the hosts' habits, schedule, and preferences. Play the games they enjoy, accept their proffered cup of tea, be attentive to their interests, make pleasant conversation, laugh with them. Be someone who enhances their lives. Be a model of honor and respectability to your sister and to all womankind. But if you're a bit boring, try running downhill.

⁂ Fanny Price: Be patient and useful to a hostess whose nature is to be a helpless slug. Be ready to help everyone in the household who needs or demands it, running errands, being obliging and unobtrusive and allowing others to feel superior if they will. Best-case scenario— your all-expenses-paid "visit" lasts forever.

⁂ Elizabeth Bennet: Be so much fun that everyone wants you around. Just-married friends insist you visit and distract them from their oddball spouses, and acquaintances invite you to balls and dinners. Women want to be you, and men want to marry you, but we don't hate you because you're just so witty. You'll be rewarded for your vivacious wit with an invitation to travel with your favorite relatives on a scenic tour of the Lake District.

In addition to staying at the homes of beloved friends and family, traveling *with* them is another way to make a low-cost, high-spirited sojourn. Don't forget that Catherine got her invitation to Northanger Abbey only because she met the Tilneys in Bath, where she journeyed with the Allens. You might likewise hop in a friend's car (carriage) and join in on a group adventure, sharing accommodations at your destination. A group trip will save you money, even if you're gracious enough to contribute to the gas and hotel expenses. Anne Elliot enjoys accompanying the Musgrove party on the trip to Lyme Regis and makes Captain Wentworth fall in love with her again while she's at it.

Making the extra effort as a good houseguest could also lead to future travel opportunities. For example, while visiting your uncle in upstate New York, you hit it off with his Siamese cat and he mentions plans to go to Anchorage in October. Offer to pet-sit and enjoy a weekend submerged in golden foliage, taking

Be My Guest

There are a few rules that every guest should follow:

Always clean up after yourself. Leave the space as tidy and sparkling as you found it, or more so.

Follow the family's preferences regarding use of windows and doors, temperature settings, pets' rules (don't hand the Pomeranian a wedge of Stilton), which room you stay in, and even who helps with dinner (don't upset the family's routine or balance of duties if it seems a task clearly needs to be done by a particular family member—you can always help with something else).

Be a harmonious presence at your relatives' or friends' home. Don't play the television loudly, even if you're watching Colin Firth bathe on *Pride and Prejudice*, or bang the pans at five A.M., even if you're mad at Willoughby, Wickham, Mr. Crawford, Mr. Elton, or snaky Mr. Elliot. Instead, keep the grandparents entertained in the living room while the meal is being prepared, or help the kids build Pemberley out of Lincoln Logs.

Invite your hosts to visit you in return, and make their stay even more memorable than Catherine's was at Northanger Abbey.

more walks in the leaves than even Marianne could boast. Make it known among family and friends in appealing places that you're open to house-sitting or pet-sitting for them in exchange for transportation. Try to arrange your travel so you can catch them at the beginning or end of their trip for at least an hour's chat over tea. Your loved ones will appreciate having a reliable person around while they're away, and you'll enjoy free accommodations while exploring the area. Just make sure the stove is off. And be sure you're alert, ultraconscientious, and good with animals if anyone's pets are involved—if you're forgetful or leave doors open, don't dare assume responsibility for another life form of any kind; Gothic nightmares will haunt you forever.

The Working Vacation

If someone else is already funding your trip for job-related activities, investigate whether you can reasonably and ethically combine work with pleasure. Are you allowed to go sightseeing or to a show between commitments or after the day's agenda is completed? Can you extend your trip by tacking vacation days to the beginning or end and paying for any extra nights' hotel or other expenses? Can family members accompany you? If a working vacation seems like a viable option, your trip will cost you significantly less than it would if you had to foot the entire bill yourself. But be realistic about your anticipated work schedule and energy level and about whether trying to balance work and play on this trip will be more stressful or joyful for you and any fellow travelers.

If your employer lets you use frequent flyer miles from work trips for personal travel, take advantage of this perk. Always keep careful track and be sure the airline credits each trip in your account. Research how many frequent flyer miles are required for a ticket to your intended destination and claim yours well in advance, as a limited number of seats are allowed for award travel on any given flight.

On Your Own Dime

We're not all lucky enough to be invited to stay at Northanger Abbey, and we may not be inspired to go thrill seeking in the dull town where we're sent for work. What should the savvy traveler do to travel economically when neither General Tilney nor the boss is paying? The key is to be a diligent detective and strategize on every expense.

TRAVELING TO BATH

If you're not due for a free ticket, get the cheapest airfare by taking the time to comparison shop. It usually works best to use travel search engines like Expedia, KAYAK, Orbitz, or Travelocity to identify the airlines and general rates for your destination, and then to contact the airlines directly to do further research and book your flight. The search engines occasionally offer discounted flights, but be aware that some of them also add service charges if you have a problem or have to change anything, which can add up to more than the discount on the fare. When you call the airlines, they are usually more responsive to questions and issues, though they also usually have a penalty fee for flight cancellations or changes. If your dates are flexible, take the time to insert many combinations of departure and return dates manually on both the travel and especially the airline websites. (Don't assume the airlines' rate calendars reveal all the possible rates.) The best-priced options are sometimes surprising, such as a particular Tuesday-to-Saturday trip being $100 cheaper than one with a Saturday-night stay. Also, don't assume that a flight and car rental and/or hotel "package" is cheaper than purchasing these services individually through each company—check and compare. Individual companies often offer their own specials. Regardless, if you do use a travel search engine for either a package or one reservation, be sure you know the cancellation or change policy before finalizing your purchase. You don't want to buy a getaway to a tropical island with the Admiral and Mrs. Croft, and then a hurricane hits shortly before your scheduled departure and you end up paying for an entire trip you never got to take (though the Admiral was willing to go during the hurricane and asked what you should do ashore). That's almost as traumatic as being unceremoniously kicked out of Northanger Abbey!

Also find out when and how you'll get your seat assignment before booking a flight through a travel search engine, if you want to be sure of sitting near the front with Henry Tilney (or if you're fighting with Maria and Julia Bertram for a seat by Henry Crawford, think again and pick one far from him; don't say you weren't warned!). They may not allow you to reserve your seat assignment at their site—the task may involve going to the airline's website and inputting code numbers, or you may be required to wait until the day of travel to book your seats at the airport when you get your boarding pass, two hours or fewer before flight departure. If the cheapest price is more important to you than the seat, go for it, but remember when and how to get your seat assignment if an extra step is needed.

A travel site may be most useful to you if it enables you to sign up for deal alerts and your schedule is flexible enough that you can take a trip on short notice. Great last-minute bargains on a flight or cruise do occur.

See if your workplace has discount agreements with any companies whose services you want for your sojourn and if you can use the discount for non-work-related purposes. Our employer has an agreement with a car rental company, which we can use by presenting the discount number obtained from the human resources department. Note that it is nearly always cheaper to reserve a rental car in advance and lock in your rate. Don't risk showing up at the airport and taking what you can get—they know you need the car and, like Isabella Thorpe, may take you for everything they can get, charging an outrageous price for a cracker box on wheels that they imprudently purchased from John Thorpe.

For travel to and from the airport, check whether an airport shuttle is available. Shuttles are often cheaper than taxis, but you may have to leave earlier or later than you'd like for other passengers to be accommodated. Compare rates; if you are traveling in a group, a shared cab may be a thriftier option. Some airports also offer free transport to a subway or bus.

WHERE TO STAY IN BATH

For accommodations, some online search engines and phone apps offer last-minute deals on hotel stays, but this is a gamble and you'll need a backup plan (especially if there's a major event in town when you're planning to be there and everything gets booked up). Search your destination for conveniently located options. Some hotels may offer their own free shuttle service to and from the airport or share a shuttle that makes regular runs of multiple hotels throughout the day—this may be all the transportation you need to get within walking distance of the places you want to go (and therefore may be worth paying a bit more than a cheaper hotel farther from the action—cab fares add up), but be sure to ask the exact hours and route of their shuttle before relying on it. On the other hand, sometimes cheaper motels and inns are located just around the corner from the higher-priced hotel. Don't forget to consider bed-and-breakfasts as well; surprisingly good deals can be available, especially on weeknights, and you'll get a more personalized, cozy experience with a hearty breakfast included (and sometimes afternoon tea and cookies or appetizers) for less than many hotels. Mrs. Allen would enjoy the comforts and sociability of a bed-and-breakfast (though you may shudder at the thought of eccentric companions at mealtime—what if the Thorpes are staying there?).

Finding free or inexpensive accommodations can reduce the cost of your adventure. Seek your own Northanger Abbey, as it were (well, your own laborer's cottage, anyway). You could try a temporary house swap with trusted family, friends, or total strangers through either a private agreement or a formal agency. Or, rent out your home to others and then go rent a home somewhere else of interest (for a week's vacation, or a longer stay if your work permits it). We suggest you avoid time-shares or any agreement that locks you in or must be reserved a year or longer in advance. Freely go wherever inspiration takes you from year to year, at a time that best suits your life, and stay at a nice hotel or cozy inn—perhaps at Lyme Regis (this is often cheaper than a time-share that is comparatively inferior in comfort).

On the other hand, if there's an incredible deal on a cabin or cottage at a place you know well and love (perhaps you've visited there since childhood) and you can well afford it and perhaps would even consider retiring there, buying your own getaway place might be worthwhile. Factor in all expenses related to the purchase including taxes, insurance, maintenance, and security. Would you be comfortable hiring a management company to take care of your property, and what would that cost? Could they book renters for part of the year to offset your mortgage and expenses, and how do they screen renters? How often would you actually get away to your getaway, and is that worth the cost and potential anxiety of being an absentee landlord, or would you be better off renting yourself?

Beware of co-owning a vacation home (or any property, for that matter), even with family. Navigating the maintenance and cleaning responsibilities can create bad blood (especially where there are no servants to perform such duties). Whether swapping or renting out your home or vacation place, you may want to store any valued possessions. Not everyone takes as good care of his property as Henry Tilney of his charming parsonage at Woodston.

FOOD AND INCIDENTALS FOR YOUR JOURNEY

If flying, pack your own earphones to watch a movie or listen to music, something to read, and your own food (trail mix, a cashew-butter sandwich, an apple, and a piece of dark chocolate to reward you for your good sense—Mrs. Morland would be proud). Carry your favorite tea bags with you as well—you can bet that organic green tea with pineapple and mango blend will not be offered by the airline, though you may get fresh pineapple juice at the Abbey, as General Tilney loves good fruit and prides himself in his pinery. Bring an empty water bottle and fill it at the water fountain or tap after you get through security. You don't want to be forced to buy those million-dollar water bottles at the airport gift shop. If driving, pack a cooler containing chilled spring waters (that you bought in bulk on sale) as well as perishable food choices if you keep it well iced. Consider reserving a room with a fridge and stocking it with groceries after you arrive, to save money by making simple meals for yourself. Throw a sack lunch and a couple of drinks in your bag when you go out for the day. Have a picnic at the park between activities. If your stay is longer than a few days, renting a short-term apartment with a kitchen may be a good option for you.

GENERAL TILNEY'S CARRIAGE:
GETTING AROUND TOWN

You chose a convenient location for your accommodations but still may need transportation besides walking to get to places like Woodston or Beechen Cliff. Check out your options in advance— does your destination have a free or cheap trolley system, buses, or subways? Can you split a cab or shuttle with co-workers or accompanying friends? As always, emphasize safety in all your accommodation and transportation decisions.

If you are traveling off season to a popular destination, make sure ahead of time that restaurants will be open, amenities available, and transportation easy to obtain. Otherwise, pick another destination.

FRUGAL GLOBE-TROTTING

What if you're not as wealthy as General Tilney, but you want to travel the world? You can still make your global adventure happen through resourceful planning. Consider a variety of low-cost options to offset your expenses. For example, why not stay at a monastery or convent during your European tour? Religious orders that offer hospitality host those seeking spiritual retreats, but many also welcome travelers of all faiths. They are located in beautiful rural settings or convenient urban centers in cities such as Rome, London, or Paris and offer a range of accommodations from the simplest dorm room and shared bath to luxury dining and spa amenities. Many monasteries and convents are described in guidebooks on the subject, such as Trish Clark's series, *Good Night and God Bless: A Guide to Convent and Monastery Accommodation in Europe*, and on their own or travel websites such as monasterystays.com, and reservations can often be made online as well. Research any specifications regarding whether a place hosts only men, only women, or married couples/families. Be aware of appropriate dress, any curfew, and how payments are made (cash or credit, and a set rate or freewill offering; few are free).

Hostels are not just for youth and may be another viable option for you; they tend to be cheap as well. As with monasteries and convents, hostels offer a range of comfort levels, prices, and policies. Check the Hostelling International organization and other websites, or guidebooks like *Let's Go*.

Would you be willing to work in exchange for free rent? In both the United States and other countries, there are organizations that identify opportunities for people to teach English, house-sit, labor on an organic farm or ranch, exchange hosting experiences, or volunteer for humanitarian/peace building work. Wwoof.org (World Wide Opportunities on Organic Farms), organicvolunteers.com, couchsurfing.org, housecarers .com, and other sites provide information about such prospects. Some organizations require annual membership dues and a screening process for participation. As always, thoroughly research your options and make safety your top priority. Don't stay at the home of a stranger of the opposite sex, for example.

Travel Buddies

Not only for your safety and budget, but your enjoyment as well, be sure to travel with at least one other person whenever possible. Catherine Morland, Jane Austen, and any proper lady of the Regency would do as much. You can help each other navigate unfamiliar places, split hotel and cab costs, and share adventures. It's usually more fun to brainstorm activities and exchange reactions to a desertscape or sculpture or musical or manatee or crème brûlée or scandalous flirtation of Captain Tilney with a friend than to go it alone. But choose your companions carefully. Don't count on Isabella or John Thorpe to pay a cent! Eleanor Tilney would be a much more reliable and pleasant choice, and be sure to invite along Elizabeth Bennet and Emma Woodhouse as well—they'll never be at a loss for witty observations on all your proceedings.

We bid you farewell!

Tips:

> ❧ Always ask about special rates, whether for your accommodation, car rental, a meal out, or admission to a museum or show. There may be a discount for members of AAA or a frequent flyer program, people over age 55, veterans, students, educators, lovers of Jane Austen, or personal friends of Lady Catherine de Bourgh.

> ❧ Strategize ways to achieve multiple goals in one trip—visits to family members or friends, attendance at work-related functions, and a few tourist adventures of your own, just for fun.

> ❧ We agree with Mrs. Morland's sensible advice to Catherine—pack with the climate of your destination in mind, and we beg that you will always wrap yourself up very warm about the throat when you go out in chilly weather.

> ❧ Clearly, one has to be a more clever sleuth than Catherine to plan an economical journey. But if adventures will not befall us in our own village, we must seek them abroad.

> ❧ Whenever you can, change your scene and live a novel plot of your own devising.

Chapter 11

Enjoying Life's Free (or Nearly Free) Pleasures Like Jane

". . . kindness, conversation, variety, without care or cost"

Jane Austen had limited means, but fortunately, our favorite novelist found joy in activities that cost little or nothing. Both she and her heroines relished an abundant variety of occupations that stimulate the mind and invigorate the body: clever conversation, reading, acting in family theatricals, taking walks, visiting friends, dancing, gardening, playing the piano, and writing letters. For Jane Austen, as well as for us, many of the liveliest and most interesting diversions available cost nothing at all. Jane and her heroines make excellent role models, as cultured women who embraced the best of what life has to offer, from the simplest to the most refined pursuits.

Certainly, good conversation with good friends is one opportunity to gain real joy without expending anything beyond time and goodwill. If friends are in short supply, we can bring joy to others by being cheerful wherever we are, and from those encounters, we can widen our circle of acquaintance. Like Jane and Cassandra, we can charm the hours away in being charming to others, thereby gaining enjoyment for ourselves.

Let us leave behind all our ringing gadgets with their glaring screens and become children of nature again. There is a little Marianne Dashwood in all of us that feels most alive on a long tramp through whispering trees and lush hillsides, and declares, "Is there a felicity in the world . . . superior to this?" Whether or not we share Marianne's partiality for dead leaves, we can all find ourselves captivated by nature and its many beauties—the hypnotic ebb and flow of ocean waves as they curl, peak, and roll into shore at one of the many public beaches that line our coasts. Or perhaps the clean, sharp cut of jagged cliffs or valleys alive with spring growth in national, state, or local parks. At least once in our lives, we should climb to the top of a precipice or lookout tower and take in the stunning views below, see the sublime grandeur of creation, and question, with Elizabeth Bennet, "What are men to rocks and mountains?"

Your Own Beautiful Grounds

But for thrift, you don't always need to travel far to find nature at its wildest pitch. You can get to know the nature around you, even in your own backyard. You can cultivate your own patch of earth with a garden. Even if you don't own property, you can root a sweet potato in a glass of water on the windowsill. If you buy fresh herbs for cooking, root a sprig of basil in the same way, and grow herbs on the windowsill as well. Oranges, lemons, and tangerines will make interesting plants if you put the seeds in a little earth. Lots of popular houseplants can be rooted from cuttings. Spider plants drop little plants in order to propagate, and you can easily create a new plant from those. If there is a botanical garden near you, watch for clubs or programs that are free— most gardeners will share their bounty, including rooted cuttings and seeds.

Explore the parks and gardens in your city or town; you'll be surprised at the rejuvenating serenity of a collection of spare shrubs or shy blossoms, much less the more ornate beauty of a sculptured bed of richly colored roses or the simplicity of a Japanese garden. We can host a wild garden in the suburban backyard, with little ecosystems of ponds and groves. Birds and butterflies fill the air and come to the feeders, adding their song and their beauty to the scene. Even the smaller yard of a house in town can become a natural wonder. Kathleen remembers standing with her brother on the balcony of their childhood home, scattering many packets of seeds, which mixed in the winnowing wind before landing in the small garden plot below. They became a glorious tangle of flowers and vegetables, vibrant colors, and harvest delights. When we find our piece of the planet, great or small, it brings us back to ourselves. We feel human again, grounded on this earth.

Don't forget that there's no better way to behold nature's beauties than while taking a walk. For the more ambitious, running can increase one's endorphins, which can be essential if one will be forced to socialize with the Bertram, Bingley, or Steele sisters in the near future. Joining a walking or running group or dancing class in which these troublesome ladies are not participants can be a healthy social activity. Sports teams of all types and ability levels are available in many areas, whether you are as aggressive as Lydia and looking for a serious football league or want to try Wallyball for the first time for fun (and then maybe quit as Emma would do . . .). Your neighborhood, workplace, church, or community center may have teams that welcome new members and are free or low-cost to join.

A Great Reader

Of course, our Jane encourages cerebral activity even more than physical activity as the greater pleasure of the two. She was a "great reader," as Elizabeth Bennet is accused of being, and she and her family loved to read novels, plays, poetry, and essays. Austen's loved ones were her first readers, and we will not be her last. Among her characters, Marianne, Fanny, and Anne are partial to poetry; Catherine Morland savors Gothic novels; and Eleanor Tilney enjoys history. Few of them were strangers to the paid circulating libraries of cities like Bath.

Ah, the glory of the library and the free fulfillment of our intellectual curiosity. Unlike Jane and her heroines, most of us can find an ample supply of books available free of charge at our local public libraries. The ability to take out not only books, but DVDs, CDs and tapes, magazines, and diverse other materials, depending on the library district, cannot be underestimated as a reason for having a library card. On one occasion, we heard a library patron say, "My library card is better than my credit card. When I can't afford to go shopping, I can go to the library and a whole world of books and DVDs is available to me—no cost, no interest. I love it!"

Many public libraries also offer a wide variety of free activities suited to almost anyone, such as book discussion groups, writers' circles, expert speakers, and genealogical research. Activities at the library enable participants to meet like-minded new friends—writers, dancers, readers, quilters—whatever the nature of the pursuit brings forth in an audience. Our local library, for example, offers free classes in Latin dancing, which expand our horizons socially and culturally.

At home, reading silently or listening to books on CD can add pleasure to an afternoon or evening. Like Austen and her characters, we can also read aloud to others, or we can enjoy someone else's reading. Plays often make the best group literary entertainment. Who can forget Henry Crawford's talent for reading Shakespeare, that clever cad! A friend of ours states that listening to books read aloud reminds her of being read to as a child—it gives a sense of deep enjoyment and satisfaction, especially when the reader is perfectly selected to match the text. Lady Catherine would read the role of Lady Macbeth with ponderous distinction, Captain Wentworth would recite *Paradise Regained*, and perhaps Mrs. Clay would oblige us by reading from *A School for Scandal*. . . .

The Pleasures of the Pen and the Piano

Writing makes for another stimulating, low-cost pastime. Austen frequently exchanged letters with family and friends as the main available mode of communication. Who says that letter writing is a lost art? Most people love to receive a personal letter delivered to the home or mailbox. Much better than an e-mail (another possibility), a real letter on real paper can be savored and reread; it will never be lost to a computer program update or a crashing hard drive. It can be saved or shared, as Austen often mentions sharing her sister's or niece's letters with the family circle; she tells us how much the audience for these letter readings enjoys hearing the news from family members and mutual friends. Although the price of a stamp is rising, receiving a letter is still free and sending one still inexpensive. The return for the joy of writing or receiving is still well beyond the small cost of paper and stamps.

If you've always wanted to write a novel, get started. You may not become the next Jane Austen (who could?), but you can create a memorable gift for loved ones. Write a little every day. Read your work to your friends and see how much they enjoy it. Gain the satisfaction of sharing your ideas and imagination with others. Not quite ready to do that? Start a journal and spend time each day in journaling. Use a sketch pad and sketch the world around you to illustrate what you have to say. You can turn those sketches into cards or personalized stationery to send out to your family and friends.

Playing instruments and making music were common accomplishments in our Jane's era, although not everyone can play well. Austen herself practiced the piano every day and enjoyed attending concerts. Music sharpens the mind as it speaks to the heart. Take lessons in piano or guitar or clarinet, if you have an instrument at hand, in exchange for lessons in your area of expertise or hours of cooking or landscaping. Or dust off your recorder from grade school and give it a try. Borrow your uncle's harmonica, or make your own instrument. Sing the melody that's bursting to be set free.

Playing Musical Pianos

Music stores sometimes have a lease-to-own program for finding pianos a good home (you can rent and then return the instrument when you move, or finish paying it off and take it with you). Also look for an enticing mystery clearance box of piano music that contains surprising melodic treasures for a song. For listening, good used CDs are available at many thrift stores.

Homemade Entertainment

In the mood to express your visual creativity? Experiment with redecorating your place by rearranging the furniture and rotating colorful items found around the house. Reorganize your closet, desk, or jewelry. Hang hats and necklaces in a funky arrangement in your bedroom or dressing area. Make jewelry from found items, either from nature or from all the odds and ends you can find.

The Best Company

Enjoy events that local communities offer for free, such as community band or orchestra concerts. Local universities have distinguished speakers whose presentations are sometimes given without cost. Students' music or dance recitals are free or cheap as well. Both university and community theater events tend to be low-cost, high-quality productions. Home shows and health fairs give useful information without charging admission. All one needs is to watch or listen to the community bulletin board on public media outlets, check the city or town hall for announcements, or pay attention to signs by the side of the road, installed to inform the public of these events. Call your area's art museum, science center, zoo, or gardens for special free or discount days.

Discover something new all the time; it's good for the brain and adds zest to life. Learn French, as any respectable gentlewoman of the nineteenth century would—you can listen to audio recordings from the library while you commute to and from work.

Being an interesting person will make you better company. The witty banter of Austen's brightest characters is worth reading again and again. Clever conversation is underrated by many today and may have been Austen's most cherished free pleasure. Visiting friends and neighbors was a commonplace activity, especially among women, and one was expected at least to endeavor to be entertaining company. Sparkling wit is free, and there is plenty of it to be had among Austen lovers and other enlightened people of goodwill. One need not purchase anything at all to enjoy the art of conversation. For example, imagine two ladies chatting while browsing at a thrift boutique:

LADY A: *Is this a dress, or a wall hanging?*

LADY B: *It depends upon the wearer. Would you like to try it on?*

LADY A: *Are you calling me a wall? Or a wall hanging? Perhaps I misinterpreted the metaphor.*

LADY B: *At the moment, one might call you a bit obtuse.*

LADY A: *Forgive me, but I prefer the word abstruse.*

LADY B: *Consider this suit—is there a human form in existence that would function clothed in this?*

LADY A: *If a crane assumed human form and required a suit for a job interview . . .*

LADY B: *Your premises are faulty. For one, a crane's innate beauty renders reliance on fashionable garments unnecessary.*

LADY A: *My blood sugar is low at the moment, but would not a crane in human form lose its distinctive feathered glory, thus necessitating human covering?*

LADY B: *You are assuming it would not transmute fully refashioned into a Parisian model ironically clad in a feather boa.*

LADY A: *Would the boa consist of crane feathers? Regardless, I object to the exploitation of birds for their feathers.*

LADY C: *Do you two ladies require any assistance? Can I help you with that suit?*

LADY A: *. . . Ah . . . thank you, but . . . we think it more suitable for a crane.*

LADY B: *. . . Cranes are so elegant, you know.*

And so forth. To quote *Persuasion*, "Their interesting, almost too interesting conversation, must be broken up for a time. . . ."

Attending a regional festival in your area or while traveling can be fun and furnish rich material for conversation among friends. Many festivals pay tribute to a special, local fruit or vegetable. There's even a rutabaga festival! These events usually feature a colorful parade as well as great food in which the theme ingredient stars supreme. We've sampled a rutabaga milkshake, and it was surprisingly tasty.

The Rummage Sale Racket

A common community event that every conscientious thrifter must experience is the rummage sale at your local church, synagogue, or nonprofit organization. It is often free, or costs a few dollars or a donation of nonperishable food for a food bank. When we were growing up, our mothers used to take us to church rummage sales whenever the opportunity presented itself. They would bustle around briskly, lifting items out of the piles on display with a smile of excited discovery. We learned to share their excitement and continue the tradition, and you can, too. Rummage sales are great occasions to attend with family; they raise money for valuable programs and services and bring communities into an Austen-like togetherness. And the best part is that if you love finding bargains among gently worn or antique items, you can find them there.

Rummage sales always have mysterious mountains of uncharted prospects, which often consist of shirts, sweatshirts, and sweaters for next to nothing, but you could find anything on a church sale jumble table. Better still, they frequently offer boutique rooms, with the very best items carefully hung on racks or laid out on tables for easy inspection. Gently worn and brand-new items, as well as treasured collectibles and antiques, are there, waiting for you.

Check your local paper for listings of rummage sales in the

area, and be on the lookout for signs posted in front of churches and around town. Ask your friends if they have favorite sales they attend—we have our own list of sales we wouldn't miss, and we're willing to stand in line for a half hour or so to be among the first to enter. Late fall and spring are popular seasons for these sales. Some rummage sales have a preview event the night before with refreshments and even entertainment. Ask a member of the church or organization running the sale for more information. One preview we attended turned out to be an upscale wine-and-cheese social at which wealthier customers bid on higher-priced items to the accompaniment of violin music (we enjoyed viewing the unusual wares but didn't buy anything). But a preview could also simply be an early-shop opportunity for the volunteers, to reward their efforts—many times workers at the church's rummage sale are allowed to buy a few items early as a reward (hmm . . . some of you might want to volunteer at your church's or synagogue's next sale!). People who arrive when the sale starts get the best selection, but people who buy later in the day often get better prices on what's left. If the sale is really good, you may want to go early and late to reap the benefits of both strategies. You decide.

Spending time in good company, not spending money, is what enriches our lives. By embracing the favorite pastimes of Austen and her heroines, we strengthen our bodies, sharpen our minds, and inspire our spirits. We may have been led to believe that entertainment is expensive, but really, some of life's best pleasures—friends, family, and community—are free. All we need is time and a little wit, and like Jane Austen, we can make our own pleasure.

Whatever you do, expand your horizons. Plant a tree with

Marianne. Learn English country line dancing, or how to make Bingley's "white soup." Paint Emma's portrait, or have Anne Elliot teach you basic first aid. Be like Elizabeth Bennet, and "have pleasure in many things."

Enjoying Janesque Leisure

- A good old-fashioned nap, or at least a time of quiet reflection when you put your feet up, shut your eyes, and listen to some soothing harp music (Mary Crawford's latest album), can be a total indulgence. We lead such overpacked lives that leisure disappears. Insist on downtime, for your health, sanity, and quality of life. Build it into your schedule if necessary and be unavailable, with your phone off. How else can you dream of Captain Wentworth in peace?

- Besides your local public library, the nearby college or university library may also offer membership to the public for free or at a moderate rate. Libraries often host book sales, and there are live and online book swaps to explore.

- There are many societies and associations that are free or charge a nominal fee and focus on any topic of interest you can imagine, such as Kabuki theater, virology, slow living, marine mammals, Anne of Green Gables, cut-glass collecting, or hang gliding. Find a group that intrigues you or consider starting your own. For a modest annual fee, for example, you can join a special group of enlightened individuals known as the Jane Austen Society of North America (or an Austen society where you live—there are groups in the United Kingdom, Australia, Brazil, Argentina, and the Netherlands). Jane Austen is everywhere.

Aunt Norris's Top Ten Aggressive Tips for Ferreting Out Free Treasures

Let's be honest—there's a little Aunt Norris in all of us who believes that one of the greatest pleasures in life is of the material kind: getting free stuff. Therefore, we set aside our idealism for a moment to learn from the Queen of Free how to gain something for nothing.

"What else have you been spunging?" Maria Bertram asks Aunt Norris in *Mansfield Park*, when her aunt manages to "spunge" the delicious cream cheese and other goodies on a visit to the Sotherton estate. This actually flatters the future Mrs. Rushworth, who "was half-pleased that Sotherton should be so complimented." As annoying as she can be, Aunt Norris is the master moocher, so we pass along her top ten tips on how to ferret out free treasures.

1. Get busy. Who is more of a bustling busybody than Aunt Norris? As Tom Bertram would say, "I wish my good aunt would be a little less busy!" But don't forget—that's how she gets the green baize curtain, and what reasonable woman wouldn't make an effort to get free fabric? The world is bursting with bounty, and one must be alert to any chance to claim it. Be in the right place at the right time. This means, be everywhere at once. Check all likely freebie venues regularly. Check online sites like Craigslist and FreeSharing.org if you are searching for a particular item, or just trolling for—who knows what? Check all other likely freebie venues regularly. One should always be ready to receive—keep your gloved hands open for any handouts.

2. Make congenial conversation with everyone you meet, as every genteel woman would do anyway. We can be as charmingly chatty as Aunt Norris, but unlike her, we genuinely care about other people and also find them intriguing. Thus, having affirmed our benignly sociable intentions, we must also acknowledge a positive side effect of our sociability—the people we encounter may happen to be parting with something desirable or to know someone who is. Be democratic—get to know not only the prosperous, but their hired help. They could use a friendly chat with someone empathetic, especially if, rather than working for the likes of Mrs. Jennings, Emma, or Lady Russell, they have to try to please Mrs. Ferrars or General Tilney (what happens if dinner isn't served on time?!). They also see and know much that may prove useful.

3. Flatter with flair (and sincerity, of course): The best-placed flattery can result in spontaneous acquisitions, whether an intriguing old handwritten recipe book, a pair of Manolo heels, or a set of charming Limoges china. Compliment especially whatever someone else has, does, or makes that you covet. Admire it as a symptom of his or her excellent taste or skill or general superiority of character, which, at least to some extent, it is. Pick up the item with care and hold it with frank admiration and a barely suppressed longing. If you're feeling a little misplaced self-pity over your lot in life (as Aunt Norris does when her "spunging" is especially effective), you could add a slight sigh of sorrow for your hardships that suggests that somehow, this acquisition would bring a hint of joy into your world of heroic forbearance.

As you affirm the possessors' discrimination while gently

fondling their home-dried herbs or fresh bread or lace apron or crystal vase (or all four if they're from the same source—you strive to make the most efficient use of your time and talents), they may decide that no compliment is greater than your affirmation and no honor more complete than to hand you all their worldly goods at once. You will be judged only by the results of your efforts. As much as Julia might mock Aunt Norris for "dancing about with the housekeeper," we must all acknowledge how productive her dancing was. Need we remind you that her day's work of schmoozing servants yielded not only the delectable cream cheese, but also "a beautiful little heath," four pheasants' eggs, and probably more treats that she chose not to mention (after all, she had two parcels plus a basket jammed into the carriage and knocking Maria's elbow).

4. Troll for specific items you need or want. Just be sure you offer a well-told tale of courage in a crisis. "Our _____ [fill in appliance or gadget here] was destroyed in an electrical explosion of epic magnitude and we're lucky to be alive. We're going to have to get a new one [sigh of resignation—you're so strong in the face of disappointment]. On our budget, I wish we could find a reliable one used, but that seems unlikely. . . ." Trailing off gently is an art; you must know when to interrupt your sob story. If you can truthfully embellish it with any moving concrete details, do so. For example, if someone else stole or ruined the item, all the better—it lends pathos to your tale of woe and motivates the listener to come to your aid—but keep it simple. Example: "My nephew, dear boy [plaintive look], spilled his juice box all over the [laptop/rug/DVD player/etc.]. I adore him so that I could hardly scold him for such a trivial thing . . . [look

of selfless devotion]. Indeed, for my own part, I love to see children full of life and spirits; I cannot bear them if they are tame and quiet."

It must be clear that you're merely making conversation, not hinting for a handout. Then the listener can become your hero, suddenly discovering a way to solve your problem through the sheer inspiration of the moment. He or she replies eagerly, "You know, I just happen to know someone who is buying a new ____ [fill in item] and might be willing to give you her old one. Do you want me to ask?" Act surprised at the very thought, but reluctantly agree, showing awe at the person's genius in conceiving such a plan. With close friends or in very casual contexts, it may be okay to ask more directly for what you want: "Do you know anyone who's planning to get rid of a____ [mower/dishwasher/bullhorn/disco ball/monkey portrait]?"

5. Train your ears, if you want to become as talented a taker as Aunt Norris. She hears and sees nearly everything—others have to strategize to keep anything a secret from her. Someone may casually mention plans to part with a possession in your hearing. If anyone begins a sentence, "Does anyone want . . ." be alert and ready with your mouth poised to formulate your "yes" (but do just give them the chance to name the item, in case they happen to be offering something objectionable in the form of a vat of manure tea or an ostrich or a copy of Mr. Collins's sermons). Quickly thank them for mentioning it (thus forestalling anyone else from staking a claim before you), and if it's anything you could possibly want, tactfully offer to "take a look" in case it would fit your needs/space/décor.

6. Be willing to work for your freebies. Avoid the "shocking trick" of "always lolling upon a sofa" if you expect to get good

gear and avoid a scolding from Aunt Norris. If someone offers you a dining room set, you must be willing to move it yourself (or arrange for others to move it for you). Take regular thrift tours in promising places. Cruise prosperous neighborhoods on bulk trash day (which is scheduled for specific dates in some cities, such as on the third Friday of each month), and check the roadsides and alleys for trashed treasures. Stuff placed beside garbage cans and Dumpsters is usually fair game. Whether you jump in and dig through the filth is up to you (better yet, find a Fanny Price to do it for you, as Aunt Norris would). Check the back of thrift stores as well. We know people who have found furniture that way—a nice futon was too large to fit through the rear entrance of the store and was about to be thrown out when they offered to take it (successfully disassembling it to pack in their car and then reassembling it at home).

Search for free samples at home shows, health and beauty fairs, or, best of all, sample day at the grocery store. Note: Don't treat these sampling events like free-for-alls or all-you-can-eat buffets and begin insinuating extra samples into a pocket or handbag—there is a limit, even for Aunt Norris. One sample at each station at a large grocer is reasonable and satisfying unless one is General Tilney and expects a king's feast every day at the strike of the bell.

7. Check the end of sales. One must temper one's self-restraint with openness to legitimate opportunities for bounty. In the field of free, the tail end of garage, estate, or rummage sales can be especially prolific for giveaways or fill-a-bag deals for a buck or two. We've even heard of jumbo mystery garbage bags stuffed with clothes for fifty cents, which is the next best thing to free and a fun treasure hunt in itself. Ask if there's anything you can

"take off their hands" for a bargain—people may not want to transport heavy or awkward items such as a leftover couch at a rummage sale and may even offer a desirable larger piece for free if you ask graciously. Some websites include a designated list of free stuff, and you can sign up to receive alert messages when something is up for grabs. Freesale websites focus exclusively on free items. The giveaway might announce a curbside donation that goes to the first taker or invite those interested to call for viewing and pick-up. A friend got a big, beautiful mirror by calling ahead immediately after finding the listing. But these timed grabfests can be aggressive. One must be as strong and swift as Aunt Norris to brave such a battle and bring home the prize cheese (all while appearing to be a disinterested philanthropist).

8. Look at everything with an eye to its potential. Aunt Norris saw the free pheasants' eggs she mooched at Sotherton as future pheasants and eggs. Ask yourself: Does an item have potential? Will it repay your modest efforts in its usefulness and appeal? Furniture can often become charming with a little effort and creativity. A sea-blue finish and new knobs make a dull cabinet a charming hutch that would fit right in at Barton Cottage. Painting a landscape or stencil on a table or shelf with the skill of an Elinor could transform it into a showpiece in your beautified home. If, like Maria and Julia Bertram, you lack artistic skill, take only what you'll use with simple or no improvements, or it will end up discarded to Fanny Price's attic.

9. Consider trading your discard for something you do want. You can exchange goods, services, or skills and never pay a cent, even for entertainment—volunteer as a gracious usher at your

local theater and see wonderful plays and concerts for free. We realize that reciprocity does not sound at all like advice from Aunt Norris, but if such an arrangement would be in your best interests, she couldn't object. Fanny Price makes out far better than Aunt Norris with very little effort in return—she's transported from a poor household to a rich one and supported free of charge, provided with free tutoring and horseback riding, and is set to take over the Bertram family as its future matriarch, all because she helped her wealthy Aunt Bertram with her worthless needlework projects and put up with the occasional impotent bullying (which she resisted beneath the veneer of proper feminine passivity). She gets way more freebies than her Aunt Norris by her tenacious persistence—the two of them have more in common than either would admit!

10. Make use of the people around you, whether family, friends, or strangers. We mean this in the best sense: Affirm and call upon their abilities, talents, and know-how. You will give their lives renewed purpose and fulfillment.

If there are rambunctious younger relatives about with excess energy to burn, send them on missions of delivery or retrieval and challenge them to do physically demanding tasks; make it a competitive game (pit the Middleton, Musgrove, and Hargrave boys against each other, for example). If that doesn't work and they seem to have forgotten their duty, guilt them with your age (though you are perfectly capable of doing whatever it is for yourself). Bug them incessantly so they just cooperate to shut you up (which should be a losing battle, but it's important to let them think it will work . . . meanwhile, you can concoct another task while they're completing the previous one). These days, younger people are often savvy with new technologies; we have solicited their aid with computer programs and a digital camera, for example.

You can also legitimately scavenge in your own home and the homes of close family and "borrow" items that eventually become your permanent possessions. For example, your husband's T-shirt makes a great oversized nightgown or dress with a funky belt, and your daughter's or niece's sunglasses or novel or piece of pie exactly suits your needs. Just as being of use brings you the purest of joy, it will surely do the same for your loved ones.

The richest way to "spunge" off family, friends, and acquaintances, old and new, is to absorb as much useful knowledge from them as possible. They'll be flattered by your recognition of their insight, skill, or experience and you'll be better informed (whether about kite energy, tenants' rights, or making taffy). Even strangers in the waiting room at the DMV may offer useful information, though you won't feel free to ask as many questions as you'd ask family. For example, if, like Mrs. Elton, you have just relocated to a new community, you'll want to ask longtime residents for their recommendations of a doctor, dentist, vet, lawyer, mechanic, electrician, plumber, and so on. Every time a person moves, it's a challenging adjustment building a new support team. Even if you've lived in the same place for many years, someone else may tip you off to a great restaurant or, better yet, a thrift store you didn't know about (as impossible as that sounds).

For your entertainment, spunge up as many stories as you can as well. Eavesdrop on colorful dialogues at the office, mall, library, parish hall, or temple. Or invite direct narratives by chatting up your neighbors in the waiting room at the dermatologist's. Most people like to talk, especially to a new audience, and everyone has at least one crazy tale to tell. Observe all the quirkiness around you and store up humorous anecdotes to share with friends (or to put into a novel).

For example, perhaps you overhear a group debating over who would get the cream cheese if Aunt Norris had to compete with Lucy Steele, Wickham, and Henry Crawford for it. Everyone seems to agree that Wickham would try to abscond with it in the night, but if that could be prevented, it would be a close call between Aunt Norris and Lucy. Things become rather heated when those on Team Lucy insist that she's much better at manipulative flattery, while Team Norris counters that Aunt Norris has more force of will. An unseemly ruffian suggests that Wickham disarms both women with his seductive charms and then easily usurps the cheese with their blessing, at which point the debate intensifies. But a dignified woman who is clearly the Lady Catherine of the group interjects with righteous emphasis that degenerate insinuations are a poor substitute for wit. The rest are silenced for a moment, until one holdout for Crawford claims that he swiftly disempowers all the competition through his mesmeric theatrical style, and then demonstrates by bursting into a passionate Shakespearean recitation featuring the cheese: "Is this a cream cheese I see before me? . . ." At this point, you decide you've spunged enough and tiptoe quietly away.

Whether you employ Aunt Norris's ways or take a less aggressive approach, please remember always to express enthusiastic thanks for all freebies, whether humble or lavish. If an item works out particularly well, describe its use and effectiveness in more

Aunt Norris's Strategies to Avoid

While we admire Aunt Norris's great skill at "spunging," we do caution you against a few of her tactics. For one, we don't advocate stealing. Causing someone to purchase something he doesn't need, and then sneaking off with it, is stealing. Contrary to Aunt Norris's own belief, she does not always think of everyone but herself. Secondly, lying and equivocation are not only wrong but quite unnecessary to effective spunging. For example, on the carriage ride home from Sotherton, Aunt Norris clearly implies her intention to share the gifts she has received with others. She predicts that her sister will "quite like" the cream cheese but makes no formal commitment—no magistrate will appear to ensure that she follows through on this intention, and the remark has no other purpose than to mask her selfishness with the appearance of consideration. We're not fooled. We know she'll hide it away as fast as humanly possible and devour it alone with a bottle of port that very night.

detail. The giver will be gratified and may even be inspired to hand you more goodies. Also, have a clear understanding with the giver of a freebie regarding your freedom to do with it as you choose. Never accept an item that's a try-it-and-return-it deal—this is simply too stressful and could be awkward if it gets damaged while in your possession, whether by you, a spouse, a pet, a natural disaster, or those unruly Musgrove boys. Keep the rules simple. Most people say, "If it doesn't work out, pass it on to someone else."

By the same token, don't sell what was freely given to you (or if you do, give all the proceeds to charity). This is tacky and against the implicit rules of getting something for free. Aunt Norris might do this, but you won't. Finally, always give free stuff yourself. Aunt Norris wouldn't do this, but she insists we tell you that she passes along her best wishes to all of you, and if you happen to insist on her taking any good thing you have to offer, she reluctantly accepts, but only at your earnestly pressing her with tears in your eyes and only as a great favor to you.

Chapter 12

CELEBRATING HOLIDAYS, WEDDINGS, AND FEASTS WITH THE JOY OF MRS. SMITH

". . . the choicest gift of Heaven"

Anne Elliot in *Persuasion* views Mrs. Smith's heavenly gifts as "that elasticity of mind, that disposition to be comforted, that power of turning readily from evil to good, and of finding employment which carried her out of herself." We all need activities that distract us from the problems and humdrums of our lives and take us into a happier, more beautiful place. What better activities, then, than those celebrations that mark and commemorate great moments in our own lives and those of friends, such as holidays and weddings.

Holidays

Austen loved the holidays, and her many mentions of Christmas in her letters emphasize which relatives and friends will be where at Christmas and whom she will get to see. In *Persuasion*, we see the jolly Musgrove family gathered in the kitchen, happily involved in holiday activities—special decorations, special foods, special fun. But holidays such as Christmas are most enjoyable when we plan for them, when we budget ahead of time for the expenses of the season: gifts, holiday parties where we work and socialize, travel, and home entertainment. Planning ahead helps us avoid last-minute stress and rush once the holiday season arrives and conserve both our money and our energy.

Thrifty shoppers plan and shop well in advance of the holidays. Their gifts are always selected with the other person's preferences in mind, and the good news is that the best gifts don't have to come from the priciest stores. You can make gifts that express your personality and fit exactly the spirit of the recipient, and some of the most wonderful gifts can come from church and temple holiday bazaars and rummage sales where one-of-a-kind items may be available, well under the price that you'd expect to pay for them elsewhere.

Holiday Festivals and Bazaars

Consider the enjoyment you will gain from heavenly festivals and holiday bazaars. Imagine a hall filled with autumnal crafts and treats: everything pumpkins, leaves, turkeys, apples; children bobbing for apples; adults buying wooden scarecrows for their gardens and bundles of Indian corn for their doors. Or picture chicks, bunnies, tulips, pastels, decorative trees with mini egg ornaments hanging from their branches, baskets, chocolates, iced cakes in the shape of lambs, an Easter egg hunt followed by coffee and goodies. Some seasonal festivals have a playful carnival atmosphere, with games and activities along with sales; important local celebrities and politicians may even volunteer to be the target in the dunk tank, brave souls!

And then there's the cake walk. Beware of the cake walk, friend. It will draw you in. It will become an addiction. Music is played while the participants walk in a circle along a path of numbered signs like stepping stones. When the music stops, you stop on the sign nearest you. The organizer draws a number and calls it out, and if it's your number, you get a cake! If you participate over and over to try to win, you may end up paying three times the cake's actual value, but you'll have a blast. And the cakes look so tempting, like the rich chocolate Bundt covered in coconut flakes like snow, or a giant, colorful frosted turkey or bunny or Raggedy Ann or gingerbread boy.

Fall and spring festivals certainly have their charms, but there's nothing in this world like a good Christmas bazaar. Follow the merry sound of carols and the smell of spices into the brightly lit room, where you'll find handcrafted gifts of all kinds. Cozy quilts and knitted afghans in rich reds and pine greens, decorative Christmas trees of every size and material, dolls dressed in velvet, carved Nativities, idyllic winter landscapes (perhaps a laughing family on a sleigh ride or children skating on a pond), glittering ornaments, brooches, and embellished toss pillows. Novelties such as a shiny glass block filled with white mini lights and tied up in a red-and-gold ribbon to look like a present make nice holiday housewarming gifts for friends.

Yes, there are some tacky items, such as those hideous plastic canvases covered with yarn cross-stitch and turned into tissue-box holders or bizarre-looking, barely identifiable figurines such as a set of three alien bears with blank, staring yarn eyes. When you find yourself face to face with these things, just smile at the misguided maker and walk quickly on by.

Why are church festivals and holiday bazaars so divine?

- They offer unique, handmade gifts of all kinds that have an appealing, homey charm you just don't find in mass-produced stuff from a store.

- Two words: baked goods. They range from homemade pumpkin spice breads and banana breads snugly tied with ribbon to glorious cookie assortments. They may be pre-selected and wrapped on holiday plates, or you may get to buy a can and walk along a cookie buffet table, selecting your own assortment. Either way, this is a wonderful opportunity for those of us with no baking talent or no time to have festive, tasty treats around the house over the holidays.

Wrap yourself up in the excitement, warmth, friendliness, light, and sparkle of the holiday bazaar, and take it with you throughout the year.

Holiday Church Sales

If you love kitschy holiday tableware, glasses, and plates, or if you're a sucker for crazy holiday decorations, sales at churches

held any time of the year as well as at holiday time usually overflow with the decorative wares someone else has tired of. Gather
up a collection of inexpensive festive serving pieces and platters
for those holiday food gifts you'll make for friends and neighbors. The bounty of the sale is yours—for next to nothing. You
can never have too many goofy reindeer. Build your own choir
of angels in every possible ethnic description. And the best part
is, when you tire of your treasures, you can turn around and
donate them again, potentially reaping your own benefits in the
form of deductions.

Holiday Budgeting

An important part of keeping that holiday spirit is maintaining
your budget. Budgeting for the holidays means budgeting your
time as well as your money. Just as you want to make a list of
the gifts you want to give and the amount of money you anticipate spending (even buying presents in advance and allocating
space in a closet to keeping them until it's time to give them), try
to anticipate the social events and parties you will likely host
and want to attend. You know that you can already name some
of them: the party or parties at work, clubs, or professional
organizations; family parties; and social events at your church
or synagogue. Pace yourself through the holiday season so that
you don't overextend your energy any more than you would
your budget.

Maybe you are the one chosen to host the family dinner.
Feeding large numbers of festive people can be overwhelming
on both the hostess and her bank account. Consider asking

family members to bring their best dishes so that the family can savor them in a holiday atmosphere. Make festive little paper flags to make sure that each cook gets credit—Gramma Sadie's famous chopped liver! Yaya's baklava! Auntie Harriette's bourbon taffy!

Perhaps it's time to invite your friends for some hospitality. Consider tea or brunch as opposed to dinner. It's easier on your budget and more manageable. Stock your festive table with those holiday goodies you picked up at the bazaar, or do a tea tasting with luscious descriptions of each tea and pretty cups and saucers. Troll the thrift shops or rummage sales for cups and saucers that match each guest's tastes and give them as party favors. Invite a friend to co-host with you to cut your costs in half while sharing in the joy of planning and preparation as well as the challenges of cleanup.

When you're the one invited, be the perfect holiday guest. For dinner, bring a little gift for the host. If you've put up jams or made candies, consider bringing something special that you have produced yourself, wrapped in pretty paper and ribbon. Not so handy? Unless you know a reason not to bring candy, chocolate speaks the universal language of appreciation. Let a box of truffles say thanks for you. Or if your hosts are lovers of wine, bring a bottle that you think they will like—if you're not an expert, ask the experts at the wine stores to help you make a selection. Remember, however, that your hosts usually have menus planned and are not obligated to serve the wine you bring, so don't expect it. If you're invited to an event for your own family, offer to bring something or to help the hostess. If you're turned down, smile and enjoy yourself.

Over the holidays, as always, avoid making credit card purchases you can't pay off at the end of the month. There's nothing that feeds that post-holiday depression as much as debt that stays with you throughout the year. Plan ahead, shop ahead, save ahead for your holiday expenses, and relax when holiday time arrives, knowing that everything is paid for.

Weddings

When Mrs. Bennet hears that Lydia is to marry Wickham in spite of all the warning signs of his character, she can think of nothing but the show. "The clothes, the wedding clothes!" she cries with excitement. She anticipates "how very merry" the family's next meeting with the happy couple will be, the knot tied and Lydia properly decked in new finery.

PLANNING

For many modern brides, the "big show" is the center of the wedding day. A year or more may be spent in planning and executing the extravaganza, often with an eye to outdoing all the other young women among the bride's family and acquaintance. The cost of such events can exceed the cost of a luxury barouche landau or a cottage in the country. What would Jane Austen or any of her more sensible ladies have to say about that?

We know that Jane gave an ironic nod to wedding publicity. In one of her letters, she remarks that a letter has informed her that one of her acquaintance, a Miss Blachford, has been married. She writes, "And one may as well be single, if the wedding is not to be in print." Today's brides announce not only their weddings in the paper, but their engagements as well, the cost of the message depending on its length and elaborateness. If Lydia and Mrs. Bennet had had their way, the announcement, no doubt, would be a full-page, full-color spread to show off Wickham's uniform.

Many couples send out "save the date" cards, as well as wedding invitations and announcements. These three printed wedding mailings can cost several hundred dollars, not including the cost of postage. Some even opt to buy preprinted thank-you cards, which increases the price. If the wedding is to be a large one, with more than a hundred guests, the cost of invitations and announcements may skyrocket.

Jane Austen's brides had much more simple ceremonies, and so can thrifty ladies today. Would Fanny Price even have considered a destination wedding at Sir Thomas Bertram's estate in Antigua? Certainly not. The focus of the wedding is on the meaning of the marriage. Even Maria Bertram, whose pretensions to splendor were considerable, has a wedding with just the right level of grandeur, perhaps even less than the neighbors expected. Maria's dress was "elegant," and "the two bridesmaids were duly inferior." Lady Bertram had her smelling salts to keep from fainting. Lord Thomas Bertram gave his daughter away. Dr. Grant read the wedding service with due propriety. Aunt Norris was able to mooch superior food and drink at Mansfield Park while supporting her sister's nerves.

Consider the budget for today's weddings. Couples today often feel obligated to entertain their guests in a fashion far more lavish than their personal lifestyles can bear. Because the bride's parents are frequently not in a financial position to afford such a show, the couple will sustain a substantial part of the costs, with the results that the American wedding in 2011 averaged $20,000 to $40,000, with many weddings costing substantially more. Unless the bride and groom and their families were very wealthy indeed, this figure represents a singular sacrifice for one day of ostentation. The same amount of money would pay for at least a year's tuition at a fine college, a substantial automobile, or a down payment on a house. Remember that John Thorpe's curricle including "seat, trunk, sword-case, splashing-board, lamps, silver moulding" cost only £50, compared to the out-of-sight alleged cost of Henry Tilney's mother's bridal clothes, £500. The couple may have to live with one set of parents or the other while waiting to save up enough for their own place after such an outlay.

Couples can conserve on their wedding expenses by exercising a little thrift, which certainly would have been approved by Jane Austen and her heroines. One can start with the very basics: What is more important, the meaning of the day or the extravagant show? Some couples opt for an intimate wedding with a supper for the immediate family; this arrangement means the important moment is shared with the people who care the most. Later, the families can have a reception or party for the young marrieds to share the joy of their union.

What is lost in this arrangement? The potential for wedding loot. Wedding presents were originally planned to help the young couple set up housekeeping; many young couples today have already finished training for their careers and are embarked on their profession. They may have apartments of their own with all the furniture, kitchen supplies, and linens they need.

Often, the wedding is an opportunity to extort money from one's nearest and dearest, hardly an auspicious start to a relationship.

Many people invited to a reception or party for a young couple often bring a gift just as if they had been invited to the wedding. Most family members want to show their support of the young marrieds by making sure that they have everything they need to set up housekeeping. But the bottom line is that the guests at the party will not feel obligated to weigh the cost of their present against the cost of the event, which means they may be much less stressed and more able to enjoy the occasion. The party can express everyone's joy at the couple's union without breaking the bank.

There's no rule that a wedding has to be held in the late afternoon and evening, with the reception including an endless array of hors d'oeuvres, a full dinner of the most expensive entrées (often poorly prepared in a reception hall kitchen), and a table full of desserts, followed by the cutting and distribution of the wedding cake. Even Lady Catherine might have balked at the expense of such a lavish display.

There's no rule that says the wedding dress has to cost thousands of dollars, either. Remember that even wealthy, sophisticated Emma and her party "have no taste for finery and parade" and dressed more simply than pretentious Mrs. Elton could abide: "Very little white satin, very few lace veils; a most pitiful business!" Even if the bride wants to wear a spectacular white creation, discount bridal outlets often have big sales where brides can find just what they want at a fraction of the price listed in bridal magazines or charged at retail bridal salons. But perhaps it would be better to exercise some Austenian restraint and not spend thousands on a dress that will likely be worn only once and then be out of style or dilapidated by the time the bride's daughter or niece would even consider wearing it for her own wedding.

Many women have their gowns made by a skilled friend or family member, or simply order a beautiful dress in white or ivory that wasn't intended as a bridal dress but suits the occasion perfectly and at a much lower price. We know of a bride who chose a tea-length dusky ivory lace dress with a ruffly, angled hem, which she wore with matching high-heeled lace ankle boots, and the look suited her vintage country style.

In Austen's day, weddings were attended by the immediate family. The bride would be given away by her father and attended by one or two bridesmaids (remember that Emma attended Harriet to church to marry Robert Martin). The groom might have a friend to attend him. Other family members would be standing by, their invitations having been handwritten rather than printed. Other friends and neighbors might have waited outside the church to congratulate the newlyweds. Brides often chose their wedding dresses to be worn later, and they often wore them out, but sometimes they saved their wedding slippers as a memento of the day. Everything was matched to the means of the family, and the size of the ceremony was appropriate to the taste of the participants.

After the morning wedding, the bride's friends and family would assemble for a wedding breakfast. This would give them all an opportunity to wish the couple happy. Such breakfasts involved pastries and hot breads, the most delicious and exquisite imaginable, especially if there was a French baker or chef at hand. Meats at the feast would include tongue (well, we might draw the line there), ham, bacon, or sausage, with the possible additions of game, chicken, fish, lobster, prawns, and meat pies. Raisins and sweets of various kinds would be accompanied by jellies for hot toast. Eggs would be served, and people would choose from coffee, tea, and "chocolate" (hot chocolate) as a beverage.

The wedding cake would often be a homemade affair, and it was likely to be a fruitcake of some kind, the richness of the fruits symbolizing the potential fruitfulness of the marriage. Everyone at the breakfast would feast on it, and individual pieces would be wrapped and sent to people who could not attend. Although Mr. Woodhouse doubted that the wedding cake could be good for one's digestion, everyone else no doubt appreciated its rich goodness, even Mr. Perry, Mr. Woodhouse's medical advisor whose children savor their cake from Miss Taylor's wedding to Mr. Weston.

Consider a morning wedding with a breakfast reception. Who doesn't love breakfast? If you're a really early riser, try a sunrise wedding, symbolizing the day. But if your family and friends aren't early birds, a late-morning wedding with a brunch reception will set just the right tone. If you choose an outdoor setting such as the beach or a park, the cost of the venue will be inexpensive, and the cost of the food less than a full dinner or buffet with appetizers and desserts as well as the wedding cake.

Thrifty couples today can have a wedding made by hand. We heard of a couple whose friends arranged a "potluck" wedding for them. The couple was married in a civil ceremony in the beautiful garden backyard cultivated by one of their friends. The music was provided by the wedding attendees, who gleefully played "Here Comes the Bride" on kazoos handed out to them as they arrived on the scene in their party finery. The food for the festive occasion was brought by the guests, each one offering the best dish possible, from potato salad to festive hors d'oeuvres. The main course was barbecue, prepared by the men of the party. The bride and groom were waved off on their honeymoon by a happy company of friends and family, who all agreed it was the best wedding ever.

But maybe your tastes run to something less impromptu than potluck and barbecue. More formal ceremonies have their distinct appeal as well, such as the winter wedding in which the bridesmaids wore emerald green gowns and dress gloves and carried copper hurricane lanterns down the aisle, ablaze with light. The bride floated by in a full-skirted dress that resembled the layers of swirling snow outside the snug church. Everyone danced enthusiastically at the reception, to stay warm as well as to celebrate the newlyweds.

Your special day should reflect your personalities, style, and values. It's still possible to have a wonderful wedding day on a budget. The important thing is making a plan that fits you and your family. You know you will have some normal expenses for the day, and how you plan for them will determine whether your wedding leaves your coffers exhausted.

Make a list of the essentials that you want to include and the possible ways each essential can be provided.

- ❧ Location: Church, courthouse, wedding chapel, reception hall, or an outdoor venue such as a botanical garden, beach, or public park

❧ Officiant: Priest or minister, justice of the peace, notary public

❧ Wedding clothes: Wedding dress, wedding outfit that can be worn again for women, and formal or informal clothes for men

❧ Wedding party: The couple and best man and maid/matron of honor; the couple and one or two witnesses; the couple and bridesmaids and groomsmen; the full wedding party including best man, maid of honor, bridesmaids, groomsmen/ushers, flower girl(s), and ring bearer

❧ Flowers: Simple garden flowers handpicked or provided by a friend; flowers bought from a florist and arranged by bride, family, or friends; full complement of flowers for church and reception purchased from a florist to meet the couple's specifications

❧ Transportation: The couple's car, cars of friends and family, one or more hired limousines, horse-drawn carriage

❧ Reception venue: Church hall, local restaurant, reception hall, room at botanical garden or other venue, reserved picnic area at public beach or park

❧ Food: Simple and homemade, provided by church groups; restaurant provided; or catered

❧ Wedding cake: Made by friends and family of the couple or made by the caterer or a baker

❧ Photography: Provided by friends or hired from a professional photographer (including videography). Note: We know of a case where passing around an old 35-millimeter camera resulted in gorgeous pictures and another where a professional photographer was a disappointment (all the photos were too dark). You must be able to trust your photographer(s) and clearly communicate your expectations.

❧ Alcohol: No alcohol provided as not necessary for guests to enjoy themselves, limited alcohol available for a toast, open bar

Every choice the couple makes will either increase or decrease the cost of the event. What will make the couple and their families happy and give the friends who are invited a wonderful day? What can the couple and their parents afford? As in every other area of thrift, there's no point in going into debt for an occasion that lasts only a few hours. If the couple loves one another, the memories for them and for their friends will endure whether the wedding party gathers around picnic tables or the most exquisitely decorated banquet table at the most expensive hotel.

There are many options for both the ceremony and the reception that cost nothing but make the occasion especially meaningful for the couple. They might choose to walk down the aisle together, write special vows, or include unique readings. At the reception, imagine Colonel Brandon and Marianne finally singing a soulful duet, or better yet, Darcy surprising his beloved Elizabeth by breaking into a choreographed dance routine, with Bingley, Colonel Fitzwilliam, the quizzical Mr. Bennet, and a heavily coached Mr. Collins as backup dancers!

What choices did Elizabeth Bennet make for her big day? We'll never know. Jane Austen chose to linger over details of the couple's depth of feeling for one another, their zealous care to do the right thing in writing personal letters to their respective relatives to apprise them of their plans, their united persuasion of Mr. Bennet to agree to his daughter's marriage to this very fine suitor, and the pleasure Elizabeth and Darcy had in looking forward to the "comfort and elegance of their family party at Pemberley." For Austen, the connections and the relationships were more precious, more valuable than the ostentation of the ceremony or the opulence of the wedding feast.

Of Catherine Morland's wedding, we know no more than that Catherine married her Henry, "the bells rang and everybody smiled." For most couples, a happy marriage day goes by in just that sort of flash, whether the wedding costs a fortune or a pittance. And so may it be with us, the thrifty. A day that joins two hearts devoted to one another need not be the subject of critique by any of the guests; the couple should be wished a happy day and a blissful life together.

For a thrifty and happy marriage, make plans that fit your fortune. The bitter taste of paying interest on a loan for a one-day occasion will linger long after the day is over. Remember the real purpose of the day. It's not to make a gratuitous display of clothing or conspicuous consumption, but to celebrate the joy of your love and your new life together.

As Austen wrote, everyone has a right to marry once in their lives for love, if they can. Celebrate your love by enjoying the wedding day that makes you happy, not poor, and becomes the model of mutual care and devotion for every day of the rest of your lives.

Wedding Etiquette

Write those thank-you letters right away. Etiquette demands that you thank your guests for their gifts within a month if possible, and if you want to really impress your guests, determine to write a personal thank-you note as soon as you open the gift. By the way, no matter what, handwrite those notes and send them in the mail. E-mails may be fine for informal correspondence, but nothing says appreciation like a handwritten note.

ATTENDING

What if you're one of the guests invited to a wedding? You, too, can celebrate the couple's special day while maintaining a budget. First of all, be sure to RSVP at once, if you can. Most bridal budgets depend on getting an accurate count of guests who will attend the wedding and the reception. If you say you are going to attend, don't be a no-show. If you're invited to be a member of the wedding party, don't accept if you can't bear the expense. Bridesmaids ordinarily pay for their dresses, usually dresses they won't wear again ever, so if the bride has champagne tastes and you have a soda water budget, you may want to bow out.

As a guest at the wedding, you are more or less expected to offer a gift to the bridal couple. Perhaps you are having to watch your pennies carefully. If you are a close friend or relative (and we hope you are if you are invited to the wedding), consider creating a personal gift that will have special meaning for the couple. Gather recipes from the family and create a scrapbook/recipe book that celebrates the two families coming together.

Ask people to contribute recipes and create a calligraphy recipe book with pictures of the recipe donors. If you are an artist, create a special work of art for the couple that matches their taste. Create or buy a special Christmas ornament, even a sterling silver ornament engraved with the year of the marriage, to celebrate their union. There are lots of unique and personal gifts that you can make for the bride and groom without breaking your own bank. Whatever your choice of wedding present for the happy couple, good manners require that you send it to them before the first year of marriage is over.

When it's time for the wedding, be a good guest. If you're coming from out of town and you're not a close relative, make your own housing and eating arrangements without bothering the bride and her family. Sometimes the bride's family will have secured a group of rooms in a local hotel, and if so, they will usually share that information in the invitation. And if such details aren't included in the invitation, don't be afraid to inquire. Savvy couples today often have a Facebook, wedding paperdivas.com, or eWedding site with expanded information on plans for their special day, so do a little web surfing to fill in the blanks. Don't expect the bridal family to provide transportation or entertainment for you when they are probably overwhelmed by all the wedding plans.

As a guest, remember it's the bride's special day; it's not about you. Dress appropriately for the occasion, not in an outfit that rivals the bride's. Behave yourself at the reception. Don't be the guest everyone talks about unfavorably for the next twenty years. Enjoy yourself and at the end of the day, thank the bride and her family for making you part of their celebration.

Everyday Feasts

Nothing beats having friends or family over to share food together, whether your gathering centers on a big game on television or a birthday celebration. Our Jane was a hearty eater and delighted in a good dinner; she describes many delectable menus with relish in her letters—lobster, turkey, asparagus, cheesecake, how well the meat was cooked, and how tragic if the butter was bad. But more important than the gustatory pleasure is the opportunity mealtime provides for a lively chat with our loved ones. We live in such a busy world that there is rarely time or energy for an actual sit-down dinner with anyone outside our immediate families, or inside them for that matter.

DINING WITH FRIENDS

Why not plan the occasional festive potluck? The potluck is a perfectly acceptable form of dinner party to host for friends or family, especially if you're on a strict budget. One can quickly sketch out the guest list and decide what entrée to serve (provide a main meat or vegetarian entrée and let people know in advance what it is). Then send around a food and beverage sign-up sheet that indicates the names and total number of those attending, and the rest will take care of itself (there are several online invitation programs one could use to post and monitor the invitation).

The house needs to be cleaned anyway, and it can be very

motivating to expect guests—suddenly, that lightbulb in the foyer gets replaced and the picture leaning against the toilet in the bathroom finds its way onto the wall. And you don't mind being in charge of creating a beautiful party space. Potlucks involve relatively little expense for the host (compared with providing an entire dinner and drinks for everyone singlehandedly) and enable one to invite more guests than one might otherwise have done. People will greatly appreciate your organizational skills and determination to make a social event for your fellow busy, increasingly isolated work drudges. Many people like the idea of having a get-together but the day is just too packed to stop and think clearly and take the initiative to organize something. You have done everyone a needed service by orchestrating this harmonious confabulation. You can add to the fun by making the potluck a theater party and reading a play aloud with everyone taking part. Try changing roles with each act or substantial scene (Note: Don't choose *Lovers' Vows*!). Or host a playwriting potluck group and perform each other's plays.

For sheer elegance, plan a more formal dinner party. You'll probably want to limit your guest list to a few friends and spend time thinking about the menu you might want to serve. Express your culinary talents in a spectacular exploration of food possibilities—make bouillabaisse or cioppino; create a vegetarian extravaganza, including putting the time into specially carved crudités and beautifully presented plates. Celebrate someone's birthday, even your own, with a special meal; if your culinary skills won't stand too much showing off, many small markets offer premade meals that are beautiful, tasty, and, better yet, already prepared. All you have to do is heat them up according to the recipes, and voilà! You're an accomplished chef.

Themed Parties

Themed parties can be a welcome change from the norm and create an extra stir of excitement among one's guests. Pick themes that enable guests to put together fun costumes from thrift store finds. For example, a disco-themed birthday party really brings out people's creativity and lends well to dancing (plus everyone wants to see Mr. Knightley decked in gold chains). A medieval feast with mummers would make an especially memorable Christmas party. At the holidays, a rich celebration of color, light, taste, and texture will warm the hearts of your guests and keep them in the cozy comfort of food and friends much later than they would guess. But what is time when such friends are to be met?

Create a special Regency party like the Box Hill picnic in *Emma* to share conviviality with your friends. Just don't ask them to say "one thing very clever . . . or two things moderately clever; or three things very dull indeed." It could prove embarrassing.

BRIDAL SHOWERS

Maybe you're asked to host a shower for a bride. Be sure to inquire what this will entail. Limit the number of people invited to the number you can afford to entertain. Consider a theme shower—one of our favorites is a date-night shower. Most brides and grooms are so overtired in preparing for their wedding and setting up housekeeping after the honeymoon that no one's in the mood for cooking. Guests at the shower are asked to bring gift cards for eating out or for entertainment that the newly married couple will enjoy. Gift cards from a favorite restaurant or tickets to the movies give the couple a spontaneous opportunity to go out on a date together without having to count their pennies. If the couple is setting up a new apartment, consider a shower for kitchen staples. Each guest brings a favorite recipe and the staple foods needed to make it—canned goods, flour, sugar, or whatever. The bride has an opportunity to fill the shelves of her new kitchen without a huge outlay of money.

If you decide to have a theme, don't make it so obscure that guests just don't get it or understand what to bring or so commercial that it's tacky and guests have no choice of gifts to bring. Be sure the honored bride-to-be gives guests flexibility in any gift wish list, as to both selection and price range. Share in the expenses if you hold the shower at a restaurant or have it catered at your house. If you do a potluck, allow other guests to contribute money in private only if there is a significant expense (such as a pricey custom cake or professional entertainment, neither of which is necessary to a successful shower).

A midway option is to have a caterer make the main meal, such as sandwiches and sides for a lunchtime shower, which you pick up and transfer onto your own serving plates, and you make only the dessert and coffee, splitting the total cost with a co-host. Some restaurants will deliver to your house for free, but it's always cheaper to serve everything yourself than to have full catering.

Share in the hosting with at least one other person, for social as well as financial reasons. No one person can or should have to do all the preparing and serving and to foot the expense for everything (unless it's a minimalist, small affair). Collaborate with a close family member or friend of the guest of honor. It will be more fun by reducing the pressure on you and helping things go more smoothly. One person can serve the coffee while another cuts the cake. People want to help (the considerate ones do, anyway), so if the lovely Jane Fairfax volunteers to scoop the ice cream, don't be jealous of her many perfections—just hand her the scoop.

People like to go home with party favors (preferably not plastic). For a wedding shower, think about two flowers in a small vase, a chocolate bar with the couple's names, the traditional Jordan almonds, a spice blend chosen by the couple that will be used on the entrée at the wedding meal, a pair of incense sticks, or two candles or soaps in the wedding colors.

If you think you can't host a shower or any kind of party because you just can't afford it, remember that the Harvilles are living in a humble home by the sea, but they are some of the most hospitable characters in Austen's fiction. Everyone feels instantly embraced and at home among them, and even snooty whiner Mary Musgrove is warmed by their heartfelt welcome. It's not the shelter or food or drink that matter but the spirit in which they're offered (and if you have a potluck, the guests will bring most of the food, anyway!).

BABY SHOWERS

Baby showers of today, like bridal showers, are diverse in style, guest list, and cost level. They can be formal or casual, coed or unisex, include kids or not, have a theme or not. The important thing is, of course, that they celebrate the joy of a new life. Whatever the style of the baby shower you host, we strongly recommend that you plan for the occasion to take place after the baby is born, and do not finalize the details or send out the invitations until the birth has occurred. Unfortunately, tragic losses sometimes occur, and the parents' pain may be exacerbated by memories of the shower and gifts that remind them of their loss. You can casually mention to your expectant friend or family member that you would like to throw a shower in honor of the baby sometime after his or her arrival and invite your loved one's input on the time frame and type of party.

A baby shower can be a formal luncheon or a casual cookout. The location can be a restaurant, social hall, park, or private home. The shower should express the personality and preferences of your loved one. For example, the baby shower Elizabeth and Jane Bennet host for Charlotte Collins is a women-only, no-nonsense picnic among the trees on the side of her house that is farthest from her husband's garden, and guests bring all utilitarian supplies for the little olive branch.

Keep the colors and subjects of any decorations simple and natural. Avoid a commercial character theme. It's tacky and can limit the guests' choice of gifts to bring. For party favors, vintage porcelain mini strollers can sometimes be found at thrift stores and would look cute filled with candy or trail mix. How about a chocolate spoon with a peppermint handle or a hard-candy bottle? Better yet, how about individual "olive branches," made with chocolate-covered pretzels dotted with green candy leaves?

The Entertaining Life

To keep a festive yet thrifty spirit all year round, remember to celebrate like Mrs. Smith, who in spite of her many challenges embraces each day with joy. Sharing with friends and family, celebrating the milestones of life, yet living within your budget will add an even greater blessing to every occasion. It is "the choicest gift of Heaven."

Chapter 13

MISS BATES AND THE GIVING SPIRIT

*". . . if she had only a shilling in the world, she
would be very likely to give away sixpence of it"*

There are as many ways as there are people to make others'
lives better, whether on our own or through organizations.
Jane Austen clearly affirms the giving spirit of her lovably mag-
nanimous characters and can be ruthlessly satirical toward the
selfish ones. Like her bighearted givers, we can express our generosity toward others through different kinds of giving—giving
of self or giving of stuff. Both forms have value and can brighten
our lives as well as the lives of the recipients, if our good intentions are directed and communicated in effective ways.

So you don't have to pull out a checkbook or dig into your
pocket for every charity—you have more to give than you might
imagine.

Sincerity in Giving

Give because you want to give. Have no thought of a return and expect none. It is Miss Bates's nature to give, because she loves people. Colonel Brandon gives without hope of a return, wanting Marianne's health and happiness, even if it does not include him. Darcy tries to give in secret, purchasing Lydia's honor by bribing Wickham to marry her and thus salvaging the Bennet family's respectability. Your kind actions can be a positive influence on others and inspire them to be more giving as well. Make genuine benevolence fashionable. Mentor others in finding their giving niche as you've found yours (and keep your eyes open for new and interesting ways to enlarge your modes of giving).

Giving of Self

Emma's longtime friend Miss Bates "was devoted to the care of a failing mother, and the endeavor to make a small income go as far as possible. And yet she was a happy woman, and a woman whom no one named without good-will. It was her universal good-will and contented temper which worked such wonders." Miss Bates knew that money wasn't necessary for her to reach out to others or to be happy—giving is free! People feel better about themselves and are happier when they lend a hand. In each of our circles of family, friends, neighbors, and co-workers, there are simple needs we can meet, problems we can solve, and sorrows we can soothe.

Despite her silliness, Miss Bates charms us because her

benevolence is so genuine and overflowing. She gives her whole cheery self to others without hesitation. Being a giving person is a state of being—generosity depends not on the amount of money given, but on the sacrificial magnanimity of the giver. Human beings have physical, intellectual, emotional, and spiritual needs, and there are as many ways to help others as there are personality types in Austen's novels. It helps to know ourselves, and thus to know how we can best benefit others.

Most of us probably associate "charity" with providing food, clothing, and shelter to those who need it. This is important work and one can either provide these goods oneself or offer financial support to ethical organizations that do so (we try not to skimp on donating to such charities when we're tightening our budgets). Emma brings supplies to the poor and sick in her village. Mrs. Jennings hosts the Misses Dashwood and is ready to welcome Edward Ferrars into her house for free bed and board when his own family disowns him. Colonel Brandon offers Edward employment (the parish living). Sir John Middleton provides the widowed Mrs. Dashwood and her daughters a low-rent cottage, thus enabling them to save face while living affordably and taking many of their meals at the estate house. He shares not only food and shelter but friendship with them, inviting them into his family and social circle. Giving in a discreet, unassuming manner is a special gift that shows the kindhearted sensitivity of characters like Sir John Middleton, Mrs. Jennings, Colonel Brandon, and Mr. Knightley—they all downplay their generosity and try to aid others without hurting their pride.

Meeting others' physical needs, in the modern world, can also mean literally giving of one's physical self for others. Donating blood or blood plasma involves relatively little discomfort but can make a big difference to those who need it. Bone marrow and organ donation is a unique form of generosity that involves some medical risks for the donor (and, in the case of bone marrow donation, is known to be quite painful). However, such largesse can save lives. If Miss Bates had the opportunity, she would be the first to give away a kidney and whatever else the doctors thought she could reasonably part with. Don't let Miss Bates's surface silliness fool you—she is the kind of remarkable humanitarian that we want to have around when we're in trouble, but that we'd rather not be ourselves.

GIVING TIME, COMPANIONSHIP, AND EMPATHY

Miss Bates has given her whole life to her mother. Today, she could have gone off on her own and found a job, rented an apartment, made her own friends, and created a fulfilling single life of work, travel, and social activity, leaving her unwell mother to shift for herself. But Miss Bates does whatever she can for others and acts on a deep sense of filial duty. She also nurtures her niece, Jane Fairfax, doting on her during her secret trials with selfish puppy Frank Churchill. And who but the selfless Miss Bates is willing to sit and chat with fussy old Mr. Woodhouse, freeing everyone else to have more lively fun? Mrs. Jennings and Sir John Middleton try to keep the brokenhearted Colonel Brandon entertained and away from isolation and despair. Anne Elliot visits her needy sister Mary and pulls her out of her depression and also cheers Mrs. Smith in her sickly poverty. Elizabeth makes the journey to supply Charlotte with much-needed intelligent company, though Charlotte chose a stupid husband with her eyes open. Social spice is one of Elizabeth's main contributions to others—she also jazzes up the lives of her family, the Gardiners, Darcy, and even Lady Catherine. Jane Bennet is supportive and kind and sees the best in others.

Most of us are so self-focused by nature that it's difficult to break away from Sir Walter's many mirrors and see those around us and what they may need besides Gowland skin cream! The fact is, many people have much greater emotional than physical needs. They hunger for the food of understanding. The lonely may be shut-ins living in an anonymous housing facility, or they may be friends or family sitting right next to us. We should emulate the likes of Elinor Dashwood, Colonel Brandon, Anne Elliot, and Fanny Price, in striving to be patient listeners who empathize with others and try to alleviate their troubles and anxieties.

GIVING GUIDANCE

Mentoring is a challenging form of giving that is not always welcome or appreciated. Austen's novels contain many mentor figures. Mrs. Weston tended the motherless Emma during her childhood, just as Mrs. Smith comforted the grief-stricken Anne Elliot in her youth. Aunt Gardiner does her best to be a positive role model for the poorly mothered Elizabeth and Jane Bennet, who strive to mentor their younger sisters in kind. Edmund Bertram supervises Fanny Price's education, and she then passes along her literary and moral learning to her sister Susan, and Elinor Dashwood does her best to enlighten the impulsive Marianne. Anne Elliot encourages Captain Benwick to diversify his reading. Giving others advice, whether solicited or unsolicited, can be of critical use to them (we prefer that it be solicited, but when it's not, tough love sometimes dictates our intervention anyway).

There are times when one must speak. Lady Catherine de Bourgh and Aunt Norris are the queens of unsolicited advice, and one suspects that their input is not always disinterested. But Aunt Gardiner does well to voice her concern about Wickham to Elizabeth (though his being a cad rather than poor turns out to be the main reason he'd make an abysmal husband)—she influences Elizabeth to detach somewhat from his charms, before later revelations reveal his bad character. Mr. Knightley can be patriarchal and patronizing toward Emma, but as a true friend, he's willing to tell her home truths that no one else dares to utter (and he's right about Mr. Elton's character and Harriet's best match). Similarly, Jane Bennet and Elinor Dashwood both intuit the characters of their sisters' love interests (Jane defends Darcy's character to Elizabeth, and Elinor questions Willoughby's integrity—both turn out to be right). Even Lady Catherine may sometimes provide useful information. She is, after all, a woman of precision who loves detail and even lowers herself to design shelving for Mr. Collins's closet, and who doesn't need more convenient storage?

Reader, does your inner voice urge you to speak? To approach a loved one with earnest advice? Are you drawn to mentor someone whose life crosses yours, because you possess or develop a kinship with him or her and sense that you are uniquely suited to offer the particular wisdom that is so clearly needed? If your intentions are pure and your instincts true, and it's truly all about the other person (rather than about you, Emma—you almost wrecked Harriet's life and we forgive you only because things worked out for her in the end), then proceed. But mentor someone only in the manner and to the extent that you feel equipped so to do. If you work one-hundred-hour weeks, it's best not to adopt Maria Bertram's hypothetical twins by Henry Crawford, no matter how desperately you see the need or how desperately she longs to part with them. We should do well whatever we can, be it great or small.

Sharing our skills and knowledge with others is a form of mentoring that can assist our loved ones in solving practical problems. For example, although it means an uncomfortable conversation about spending and lifestyle changes, Lady Russell forces herself to try to help the Elliots extricate themselves from debt, drawing up plans with Anne's input (they're ignored, but at least this paves the way for the move to Bath). Captain Wentworth uses his knowledge and contacts to help Mrs. Smith get her property back, thus rescuing her from near-penury. Anne's quick thinking saves Louisa's life, and her steady nursing restores young Charles Musgrove to health. Elizabeth's blunt communication leads to Jane getting her man back and Elizabeth getting a reformed man of her own. Even boring but patient Fanny Price repeatedly disentangles Aunt Bertram's needlework.

Fixers are valuable members of society—they tackle others' obstacles and dilemmas with gusto and do their best to eliminate them. Undertake problems you think you have the ability to solve, and teach people skills you possess that will enrich their existence. For example, a co-worker who is a master gardener is always willing to answer questions about what to plant, where to plant it, and how to take care of it. A nutritionist shares healthy recipes with neighbors. Are you a mechanic, lawyer, historian, pastry chef, business owner, osteopath, crafter, speechmaker, counselor, computer tech, hairstylist, upholsterer, haberdasher? Do you know how to operate a backhoe? Are you well informed in any field? Someone needs your input in precisely that area, and your generosity in giving it will make a positive difference in that person's life. And who knows? You may indirectly save a tree, computer, car, party, business, marriage, or even a life.

GIVING EXPERIENCES

Give yourself a treat while you're treating others—invite someone to share in your activities, plans, adventures. Got an extra seat in your carriage and an extra room in your house or rental? Catherine Morland is thrilled to join the Allens on their trip to Bath, where she accompanies them to plays, concerts, and assemblies. If you farm, let a friend ride in the hay wagon (Marianne Dashwood would love this). If you have an extra ticket to a concert of romantic operas full of love songs, invite Anne Elliot to join you, or better yet, give her and Captain Wentworth each a ticket separately without telling them you won't be there and then he can declare himself that much sooner! If you ever have tickets to any cultural event that you aren't able to attend, give them to someone else to enjoy. If you have an annual membership at an art museum or botanical garden, see if there are special rates for your guests, and if so, Harriet Smith might benefit from the opportunity. If you are yourself performing in a group and receive free show tickets, be sure to offer them to whoever would most enjoy them (if you're in a political comedy troupe, for example, invite the Palmers—he'll find it amusing and she'll laugh, whether she gets it or not).

GIVING APPRECIATION

Miss Bates overflows with gratitude to everyone who does anything for her, from the smallest to the grandest gesture, and she means it. Express genuine gratitude to others for the ways in which they've enhanced your life. This is such a simple but gratifying way to affirm people, who need to feel valued and appreciated. People are insecure; they want to be better than they are, and they get a boost from knowing that the good they do is noticed and beneficial to others. Such positive reinforcement will encourage their best qualities.

Never forget others' acts of kindness to you. Thank them verbally and also in writing with a formal thank-you card. Remember that the actual paper thank-you card, which one places in an envelope, stamps, and mails, is always most welcome to the recipient and will never become obsolete. Preferably, send one with a Jane Austen quote and miniature portrait on it.

GIVING JOY

Bringing good cheer is a special gift, and Miss Bates has it. There is so much suffering in the world and it's easy to get worn down by the struggle of living in a fallen universe. Silliness is a much-needed and undervalued quality. Pure-hearted laughter is infectious and buoys up the downtrodden. Miss Bates shares a wealth of smiles and well-wishes with all her acquaintance. She openly laughs at herself and good-naturedly giggles with others, but she never laughs at others in the mean-spirited way that Emma must learn is never justified. Miss Bates never causes others sorrow or pain for any reason. Whether one is in a bad mood or has been too indulged or has become impatient with others' foibles, it is never okay to vent our aggression on others. Austen does not allow us excuses for meanness at any time or for any reason. We are justly reproved. We will mend our ways.

Like Miss Bates, Mrs. Jennings and Charlotte Palmer love people, love company, love life. They are determined to be happy and are not dependent on circumstance for their state of mind or way of treating others. All three of these women bubble over with merriment. They are a blessing to all their friends, and everyone is their friend. Those of you who lighten others' loads, who share your genial smiles, who laugh at yourself and with others, who tell the perfect humorous anecdote to divert the person who you sense is anxious or depressed—thank you. We need you. You are a precious gift to all of us ordinary, mopey mortals.

GIVING SPIRITUAL SUPPORT

Praying was, is, and always will be free. Remember others and their life challenges in your thoughts and prayers. You may want to keep a list of names handy by your bedside or reading chair.

Developing the Giving Spirit

The giving spirit can be taught, if a person wants to learn it, so there's hope for us. For example, start with a simple exercise. If you invite guests on a walk in a scenic area, stroll along at their chosen pace and make the experience enjoyable and leisurely for them; don't launch into a speed-walk race with them in a sudden fit of misplaced competitiveness. Allow your companions to speak freely and be a patient listener, even if you're a bit bored.

You can gradually increase the difficulty of your giving exercises. Suppose you've just finished dinner at a restaurant where you're getting two meals for the price of one through a coupon special—do you still tip the server based on what the undiscounted total would have been? You should. Unless the service is poor, tip well—this is a social gesture of appreciation for the service rendered, as well as a supplement to the person's moderate income (if you're not sure whether tipping is appropriate or allowed in a particular context, ask).

Another example: You're out shopping for a box of chocolates to bring a stressed-out co-worker for his birthday. You reach for the cheap, gaudy box out of habit, but pause for an Emma-like revelation. You recall that the cheapo box is packed with a repulsive variety of inedible creams and horrific alien jellies and only a few tasty bits. You come to your senses and drive to the specialty chocolate shop after a busy day at work and personally pick the combination of handmade dark and milk chocolates that your officemate will most enjoy. You swallow hard when paying the bill but are happy in the knowledge that he'll love his gift and relish every bite, reaching for each chocolate without fear or trepidation or cutting it open for inspection first. In other words, there are times when one should reject the cheapest route and spend comparatively more money than is strictly necessary or expected, in order to fulfill a desire to support or celebrate someone. There is sometimes more value in bringing joy to friends than in saving a few dollars by scrimping on a gift.

Volunteering

Another way to develop your giving spirit is through official volunteering in a context in which you're supervised and mentored in ways of helping people. Being told whom to help and how can be a reassuring foundation from which to discover your own observations, ideas, and initiatives on how you can best meet people's needs. It's not about spending money, though financial donations help and have their place. It's about improving life for others and yourself at the same time by giving in a spirit of pure-hearted authenticity.

Match your personality, tastes, and talents with the right form of giving—do what you do well and enjoy, and help others doing it. Perhaps Emma would serve at a soup kitchen, and Marianne would be a guide at a kids' wilderness camp. Colonel Brandon would teach a community education course in dueling, while Edward Ferrars would offer an assertiveness training workshop. Miss Bates is clearly good with the elderly and would visit retirement homes for a friendly chat. It benefits all of us to spend time with older people, whether through volunteering or in the course of our daily lives. They have valuable wisdom and experience to share. When we draw them out and listen to their stories and perspectives, we learn about the past in a way no history book can teach. In the process, we often learn about ourselves as well, and what we could and should be.

Once you've developed your giving spirit, you can look around you: What do people need? Shovel the walk for an elderly neighbor. Pick up groceries for the sick family across the street. Volunteer to call or visit someone who lives alone and would enjoy contact with the outside world. And don't neglect to call your own family and friends—stay in touch with loved ones far or near that you don't get to see very often, so they know you're thinking of them. Have real, focused, cheering conversations with them. Those who have unlimited calling plans have no excuse not to call long distance. You're allowed to do menial tasks while on the phone only if (a) you are truly able to keep your mind focused on the person and conversation; (b) it's a long call; and (c) you don't make any noises that reveal that you are multitasking (no clanging of the washing machine or sawing sounds).

Thank You, Jane!

Jane Austen gave us six brilliant novels to reread throughout our lives and from which to learn so much about how life should be lived. She understood true munificence, as is clear in her creation of characters like Miss Bates, who love others with their whole hearts, even at risk of having them broken.

Austen gave us the six novels that only she could write. Give of your own uniqueness. What are your greatest talents? Your most appealing quirks? Give to others what you sense they most need and appreciate about you, whether your nurturance, joviality, suspenseful storytelling, effectiveness in fighting for others' rights, or ability to compose a clever impromptu satire on the injustice of your friend's workplace experience, until she can't help but break out laughing.

Life is hard, as Miss Bates certainly knew. Bring the kind of relief to loved ones and strangers alike that only you can give them. Every day is a chance to make the world a better place for someone. A chance to be, like Miss Bates, so very obliging!

Chapter 14

AUSTEN'S RULES FOR REFUSING, ACCEPTING, AND GIVING GIFTS

Say No to the Gift Horse, Marianne!

Not only can we give of ourselves through innumerable benevolent gestures, we can also oblige others through the more material gift of goods. In Jane Austen's world, a gift should be freely given and freely received. It should be offered with purity of heart and bring nothing but pleasure to the recipient. No conditions, obligations, responsibilities, hidden messages, awkwardness, insult, guilt, or pain. These principles may sound obvious to you, O Discerning Reader, and easy enough to follow, but perhaps you are not like Marianne Dashwood—prone to give and receive impulsively the wrong things at the wrong times. This can create a dangerous web of social and romantic ties that entrap the unwise. To avoid such entanglements and to give and receive nothing but unalloyed joy with tokens of affection, simply follow Austen's rules.

Gift Giving Dos and Don'ts

Our Jane put thought into the presents she gave to family and friends; she did her best for others on a tight budget through her wits. So did her characters. Elinor made the time and effort to paint a pair of beautiful screens for her sister-in-law Fanny Dashwood, though Fanny didn't deserve them. Give gifts that your loved ones would appreciate (even Fanny has the good taste to openly admire the screens until she fears her mother's ire). Be observant of what they need as well. Edmund gave Fanny Price a chain that he noticed she lacked for her cross pendant (and, being in love with him, she took it though she already got one she didn't want from Henry!). Mr. Knightley sent the impoverished Bates family a basket of fresh apples. Even our Jane received practical gifts from family members, which she was happy to get. Try to give items that the recipients will use that also express something about them—their taste, style, personality.

- Some things are too utilitarian to function well as bona fide presents, such as vent covers or a new tire, unless the vent covers are designed to resemble shark jaws or the tires are purple.

- Undesirable castoffs go to the junkyard. If you don't view your loved ones as Dumpsters, don't give them broken, ugly, useless, hideous rubbish.

- Don't give or request gifts that violate a person's character or beliefs or exceed his or her means. Thus, you don't hand your environmentalist best friend a beautifully wrapped tank of pesticides, or ask your feminist aunt to buy you a frilly apron and matching pumps to wear while cleaning the oven.

❧ Give generously on special occasions. However, it's still acceptable to be economical in one's generosity. Thus, one can use a 20 percent off coupon when buying the complete cookware set for a wedding gift, or get the birthday gemstone earrings and matching necklace on clearance or the drill on a promotion sale. Of course, planning ahead for major gift purchases makes finding a discount more likely.

❧ Do you still have a gift card that you never used? Yes, you can spend it on a present for someone else. No one will know. This can be especially handy near the end of the month.

❧ It's fine to give thrifty gifts if the recipient isn't known to be averse to them (but if he or she never steps foot in a secondhand shop or buys anything even barely used, you must respect that).

❧ New or used, select something that seems intended for the person, not a gift for you masquerading as a gift for someone else. Focus on others and what makes them special to you.

When shopping, get in the habit of scanning for things that bring to mind a particular person in your life. Your brother gets the vintage fish service you spotted at the rummage sale; it comes complete with rainbow trout platter and each plate featuring a different species. Your hippie neighbor gets the green shirt with the glitter peace sign on it, and so on.

It's a cliché, but it really is about the thought—show how well you know the person and the effort you invested to find or make something that reflects her or his character. Choose economical gifts that uniquely suit the recipient.

This means it's fine to give your co-worker the $1 bow tie that you fished out of the tie basket at the charity thrift store where it landed (new and unworn with the tag still on it, simply because no adult male except your co-worker still wears bow ties on a regular basis—how Selena would stare if Mrs. Elton told her of it!).

The $5 retro necklace you found on the bottom shelf at Goodwill's hodgepodge jewelry counter, with its bold two-tiered strings of deep-red beads with swirls of gold reminiscent of old-fashioned marbles, will look stunning against your friend's olive complexion, and she happens to have a penchant for fun, chunky jewelry.

What about thrifty gift ideas for casual acquaintances? When you don't know someone very well but want to make a nice gesture, here are some top picks for thrifty giving:

- ❧ A classic vase of flowers. A surprising diversity of attractive vases in a variety of sizes and designs are readily available at garage sales, rummage sales, and the cheapest thrift stores. Keep some around to make quick bouquets when you discover it's your boss's birthday or your neighbors' anniversary. It's remarkable what a beautiful, inexpensive gift you can make from an ornate peacock vase you picked up for $2 and a two-for-$10 mix of flowers and leafy accents. Or the fifty-cent clear vase you painted in a simple, abstract brushstroke of bright red, orange, and yellow and decked with blooms from your own garden. Supplying a vase yourself saves you money that you can spend on nicer flowers at the grocer (there's a significant markup on arrangements that are already placed in vases, no matter how ugly) and arrange with your own touch to make the gift more personal and attractive. The bouquet will look more expensive than it was, and the recipient will be pleased.

❧ Home décor with simple appeal. A set of multiple amber glass candleholders from a restaurant may appear on a thrift-store shelf; give them as outdoor lighting with a bag of tea lights.

❧ Gift baskets make wonderful gestures for anyone. Baskets abound in the world of secondhand. Look for a clean, like-new one with a tight weave and charming design, and then insert coffee or tea and scones and the universal gift: a copy of *Pride and Prejudice*. No time like the present to introduce new fans to our Jane. Theme baskets are enjoyable to prepare and to receive. What college student wouldn't appreciate a "late night of study" basket filled with coffee, treats, bookmarks with literary quotes, and some eccentric erasers?

Gag gifts are acceptable if you know the recipient well and the gag will be understood and enjoyed. It would be awkward if one opened an ornately wrapped box to discover a jar of bootblack or an enormous gummy pterodactyl or *Harriet Smith's Book of Easy Riddles* or a Charlotte Palmer bobblehead and was at a complete loss. The item must be hilarious and give them a real kick rather than confuse or insult them. However, a gag gift doesn't count as a person's bona fide birthday or Christmas present (they're extras or something to give in the off-season).

There is a gray area, however. Something really funky that you know your friend would like isn't necessarily a "gag" gift at all for them. A Tweety sweatshirt or a flamingo phone or a War-holesque painting of staplers or a bust of Colin Firth as Darcy may be exactly what she wants.

The incidental handoff is another option for token gift giving. If you paid little for something and are unsure whether the person would like it, you can offer it, unwrapped, as the most casual of gestures. Example: "I'm planning to part with this _____ [quill pen/rhinoceros coat rack/gypsy skirt/Marie Curie statue/alligator puppet/pair of clown bookends] because_____ [you don't have to give an excuse, but you can if it's colorful]; do you have any interest in it before I give it away?"

Mission Gift-Possible: Let's say you witness your sister admiring something at a store. Yes, it's okay for you to go back later to buy it for her as a gift. But don't do this often, or the person will become self-conscious about noticing anything while out shopping with you; it will also seem like you don't have any imagination, and no loyal Janeite would want that!

Joint or group gifts can be a great way to pool resources and plan a special surprise for someone. Jane and Cassandra often gave united gifts to family members. This is a good strategy in a bad economy and can make the present especially festive and celebratory. It's usually best for all involved in a combined gift to donate the same, agreed-upon amount (choose an amount you're confident everyone can afford). People want to feel equally involved in a gesture and fear not knowing what's an appropriate contribution.

For eco-friendly gift wrapping, try to recycle something you have, such as the traditional funny papers, or make your own gift wrap by decorating brown paper from a paper bag with non-toxic, water-soluble ink and stamps or paints. Tie with natural ribbon or twine. The recipient will appreciate the effort and creativity you put into the packaging as well as the gift itself.

Rules for the Recipient

What if you're on the receiving end? In an ideal world, one would never need to say no to a gift because only appropriate gifts would be offered. However, because Willoughbys and Mariannes continue to exist among us, we must clarify, with Austen's help, under what conditions one should refuse or accept presents as well as the etiquette for doing so.

WHEN TO SAY NO

Ladies, learn from Marianne's mistake—never accept an expensive gift from a man to whom you are not engaged, even if he is quite dashing and always carries a copy of Shakespeare's sonnets with him. If he offers you a horse, you must firmly though politely refuse it, without the need for a wiser sister's intervention. No to all gifts that create an obligation for you, especially when the man's romantic overtures are an unwelcome surprise (like Fanny Price, you cannot and will not like him, and are very sorry—or not!). Sir Thomas will have to accept that you are the best judge of your own heart.

Receiving a gift should not be stressful or complicated. It should not feel wrong or embarrassing or pressuring or in any way contaminated, and if you feel vaguely defensive about accepting it, don't. Self-respect should tell you that no serious romantic gesture should be either given or received without an engagement. Willoughby dares to hint to Marianne without proposing, to offer her a horse merely with the insinuating remark, "When you leave Barton to form your own establishment in a more lasting home, Queen Mab shall receive you." This is the act of a would-be seducer—an empty gesture, a symbolic purchase of her love without a commitment. No woman's love should be for sale. Willoughby demeans Marianne in offering the horse, and she demeans herself in her eagerness to have it. She wears her heart on her sleeve and play-acts an engagement that doesn't exist, with a man who doesn't value her enough to love her honorably for life.

Don't accept the following unless you're engaged:

- ❧ A horse or other expensive pet (assuming you can jointly afford its care and embrace the shared responsibility—but remember that an engagement can be broken and you may be stuck holding the bridle alone)

- ❧ A lock of his or her hair (and don't give a lock of yours, either)

- ❧ For women in particular, pricey jewelry of any kind, whether the cliché diamonds or anything else (you might even want to stay away from the cubic zirconia that Wickham tried to pawn off on you, just to be on the safe side . . .)

There is something almost primeval about a woman receiving jewelry from a man; it has profound resonance and must be carefully considered by both parties. Mary Crawford tricked Fanny Price into accepting a necklace from her that was really from her rakish brother Henry; this entrapped Fanny into the appearance of romantic interest in a cad—a particularly insidious female betrayal. Fanny was right to be suspicious of the Crawfords. Gifts from honorable people are untainted, uncomplicated, positive gestures that reflect sensitivity to the receiver's feelings and cement bonds of caring. For both sexes, not accepting expensive presents from someone to whom one is not engaged shows a scrupulous conscience. It's best to be honest and send an accurate message to the other person about the status of the relationship and one's current level of commitment. Get to know the person's true character over time, shunning premature intimacies. Avoid being the one dumped with phrases like ". . . if I have been so unfortunate as to give rise to a belief of more than I felt, or meant to express, I shall reproach myself for not having been more guarded." A woman only "likes" and "esteems" a man until he proposes. Call us old-fashioned if you will; we side with Elinor on this. No horses or locks of hair change hands without a ring and a public engagement. Integrity is still fashionable. So much for the rules of romantic gift giving between the sexes.

Don't accept the following from your beloved unless you've just returned from the altar:

- A house or other real estate (including an estate in the English countryside—sorry!)

- A car (or carriage, if you will)

- A cruise or other travel adventure (if you've married Captain Wentworth, okay!)

- Something of great sentimental value in his or her family, such as a grandparent's ring or antique cherry desk or wooden golf clubs or silver pinking shears or complete set of original Austen editions. They belong in the family.

Don't accept the following presents from anyone, female or male:

- No giraffes. You have a right and obligation to reject gifts from anyone that come with financial or other responsibilities you cannot or do not want to fulfill.

- Don't give or receive "trick gifts" (deceptions that are not innocent fun) or "toxic gifts" (not really a gift but a negative message from the giver).

- In general, no conditions or return requests: a gift isn't a book from the circulating library, and it's not a gift if the giver wants it back, so don't accept anything significant that's offered "on loan." If you're the giver in a special circumstance, make any reasonable condition on an item up front when offering it (such as telling your niece, "This brass lamp was your great-aunt's and belongs in the family, so I'm offering it to you first; if you don't want it or wouldn't keep it to pass on, I'll ask one of your cousins next").

If you're surrounded by reasonable friends and healthy relationships, gifts will be a natural, happy part of life. Your instincts will tip you off if something isn't right. But you'll know you're overreacting if a casual acquaintance hands you a stick of gum and you respond in a panic, "No, indeed, you must excuse me. I cannot take this. It would be absolutely impossible for me. I could not possibly chew your gum if you were to give me the world."

WHEN TO SAY YES

Reasonably priced presents from close family and friends are generally welcome. Family members often ask for suggestions—you may request something in a modest price range that you know they can afford, such as a book you've been wanting to read, a new slow cooker to replace your broken one, tools, or poetry and piano music. They want to give you what you're sure to enjoy. As long as you don't pull a Lydia and send wealthier relatives letters begging for money, with the lame tack-on that it's okay not to if they'd "rather not." Riiiight.

Say yes to any straightforward presents from family or from friends whom you like and see yourself continuing to befriend. The same gift can be appropriate from one person but inappropriate from another because it means something different. For example, a man who has unwelcome romantic feelings for you offers you a valuable gemstone ring—no way. But if an older female mentor wants to honor you with such a ring and assures you that her sisters didn't want it, you accept, and it brings you both joy as a memento of your mutual regard.

Etiquette for Getting and Giving

The etiquette for accepting a gift is simple: a genuine "Thank you." You can add a sincere compliment about the item as well, such as the neutral "How thoughtful," or "This is just what I needed." Or, if it's true, proclaim, "You must allow me to tell you how ardently I admire and love it!"

Refusing a gift is a bit more delicate. You can make a practical excuse, if relevant: "I'm afraid I have nowhere to keep a horse/giraffe/spider monkey at my condo complex." You can use a traditional script of decorum, such as to someone you're dating: "I appreciate your generosity, but I can't accept this estate/diamond/coach and six" (a true gentleman understands the phrase "I can't accept"; a cad will act baffled). If a relative or platonic friend offers you something of value that simply isn't for you, state honestly, "It's so nice of you to think of me, but someone else would make better use of that, since it's not really my taste" (you might suggest a mutual friend or relation who you think would like the item and whom the giver likes).

In general and especially among friends, give the price range of gift that you know the receiver can afford to reciprocate and likewise accept the value of gift that you can approximate. Exceptions are significant differences of income (even so, the wealthier party shouldn't give something extravagant to the less prosperous family member), parent-to-child presents, or family members gifting a loved one during a time of health crisis, financial struggle, or another major life challenge. Beyond such instances, it just doesn't work when one person gives a new Mercedes and the other gives peanut brittle.

There is no mathematical equation to the art of giving and receiving, but the gift should feel right and spread happiness to both the giver and the getter. Austen wants us to love, honor, and cherish others, and our tokens of esteem should express those precious sentiments to them.

Chapter 15

REPRIORITIZING OUR LIVES
AND ALWAYS HAVING IT ALL

Being Like Jane Austen and Her Best Heroines

As Mrs. Jennings always knew and Aunt Norris never learned, people are our most precious gifts in this life. When we follow Jane Austen's philosophy of thrift, which she has graciously passed down to us through her novels and letters, we find ourselves refocused on what matters most. We gain honor, inner peace, and happiness by paying our debts, helping friends and strangers, contributing to and bonding with our communities, preserving the earth, and having wholesome fun. By returning to the basics and embracing the many simple pleasures freely available to us, our lives are made rich in the best sense. And even if we were money-rich, we could never give up the cheap thrills of thrift shops, rummage sales, repurposing, and the occasional innocent spunging! We appreciate and make the most of what we already have, and find our joy in our hearts and homes rather than in forever looking elsewhere, and buying, buying, buying. We'd much rather be reading, reading, reading Jane Austen, and spending time with real as well as fictional loved ones.

Share and Share Alike

Once we realize we already have everything we could need or want in our circle of family, friends, and pets, how do we best strengthen these cherished bonds? We build community wherever we can and embrace a lifestyle of sharing, mutuality, and collaboration. Jane and her sister Cassandra shared a bedroom, personal belongings, travel adventures, a social life, letters, anecdotes, thoughts, feelings, and convictions. They supported one another through challenges and disappointments and took pride in each other's accomplishments. Moderate lending, borrowing, exchanging, and pooling of resources can help cement our ties with family and our local communities. Bartering has an old-time appeal. How refreshing to get and give what is wanted without any exchange of money! What about offering guitar lessons for math tutoring, or chickens for produce? The possibilities are endless. Make clear, fair exchanges that balance the participants' investments of time and skill, with some consideration for market value. In a less formal way, we experience reciprocity in our true friendships all the time. Someone spends four grueling hours patiently teaching you how to use a sewing machine to make a simple handbag, and of course, you help her pack and hold a garage sale when she's preparing to move. There are many simple ways to share with others every day. Why not pass along your magazine to your next-door neighbor when you've finished it?

We should develop and share our creativity with others as well, as Austen did. Learning new skills and abilities and stretching our powers of invention are good for the brain and pay tribute to our favorite author. Many adult educational opportunities are available at various venues in your area, such as at your local community college, public library, arts center, or area business. Check out the ballroom dancing school, bead shop, or hardware store. Explore something completely new to you and discover a talent you never knew you had while meeting new people. Imagine Caroline Bingley and Louisa Hurst high-stepping it as they learn country line dancing and hobnob with "rustics" in jeans. Perhaps Jane Bennet, Jane Fairfax, and Anne Elliot meet at a kickboxing class and discover the power of releasing all those pent-up frustrations (once the instructor convinces them that the punching bag will in no way be harmed). Lady Catherine studies Spanish in hopes of telling a larger percentage of the world's population what to do. Meanwhile, her daughter Anne "The Crusher" de Bourgh joins a gym to train as a power lifter and gets so good that she competes as part of a team. Mrs. Bennet and Mary Musgrove hit it off at a seminar on medicinal herbs at the botanical garden and become rather competitive in exchanging war stories of their illnesses. Mrs. Elton signs up for a basket weaving workshop, but strangely, the other names on the list are withdrawn and no one else has signed up yet . . . but we must nonetheless affirm her gesture toward self-improvement in venturing into the unknown.

However we choose to expand our horizons, as Austen lovers and thrift enthusiasts, we are idealists by nature. We keep going back to Austen's novels for pleasure and enlightenment and always find something new, as we keep sifting the thrift in search of unforeseen delights. We learn the best and worst in our natures through the best and worst in Austen's characters, each of whom shows us a piece of ourselves. And we do the best we can with what we have, for ourselves and for others, striving to live gracious and giving lives of festive frugality in harmony with earth, sea, and sky.

Dearest Readers, we thank you for taking this journey with us. Our Jane always brings people together, both in fiction and reality, and we all seek to follow her example of witty, pretty, thrifty liberality. Surround yourself with kindred spirits bonded by mutual affection and shared sensibility (and a shared passion for thrifting, of course!). How about three or four families in a country village? Like Elizabeth and Darcy, we can create a comfortable community of our favorite relatives and friends who understand and bring out the best in us, and they are always with us at Pemberley.

Acknowledgments

We would both like to thank our editor at Berkley, Andie Avila, and our agent, Sally van Haitsma, for their hard work and enthusiasm for this project. And we thank Jane Austen for providing the inspiration for it.

I would like to acknowledge all the people to whom I owe my insights into living well:

My mother and father, Elizabeth and Charles Wyman, who knew how to live well through thick and thin.

My sister and brother-in-law, Lisbeth and Richard Whiting, who have demonstrated how to raise three wonderful children in a challenging world.

My beloved nieces and nephew, who are the proof of their efforts: Lisa Wieczorek, Chuck Whiting, and Harriette Leitman.

My cousin Elizabeth Elliott and her husband Jerry, who have shown how the thrifty life and hard work can create a bounty of generosity, hospitality, good living, and great kids.

My dear friend from first grade, Emily Norman, whose wonderful family demonstrates the virtues of a thrifty life.

My beloved friend Bobbi Fulton, with whom I have spent

many happy hours on the garage sale trail, and her husband, Charlie, who knows how to make money grow.

My "kitty cousin," Sue Vickerman, and her husband, Ray, who are two of the most wonderful people in the world.

My late friend Janet McFerren, who showed what a spiritual life well lived can produce, and her sister Nan McFerren—"where shall we find . . . a kinder sister, a truer friend?"

My friend Linda Moody, who is the icon of New England virtues: hard work, thrifty life, generous spirit.

The late Edith Jones, who knew a thing or two about thrift.

—Susan Jones

I would like to thank my mother, Mary Theresa Anderson, for being the model of elegant economy.

I would like to thank my father, James B. Anderson; my brothers, Tim Anderson and Mark Anderson; my sister-in-law, Sudha Prathikanti; and my aunt, Jane Neuhaus, for their love and support through the years.

I would like to thank all of my family as well as my friends and students for enriching my life in many ways.

—Kathleen Anderson